Frederick Christian Würtele

The English Cathedral of Quebec

A Monograph

Frederick Christian Würtele

The English Cathedral of Quebec
A Monograph

ISBN/EAN: 9783337327002

Printed in Europe, USA, Canada, Australia, Japan

Cover: Foto ©Lupo / pixelio.de

More available books at **www.hansebooks.com**

THE

ENGLISH CATHEDRAL

OF QUEBEC.

A MONOGRAPH

BY

FRED. C. WÜRTELE.

QUEBEC:

PRINTED AT THE "MORNING CHRONICLE" OFFICE.

1891.

THE ENGLISH CATHEDRAL OF QUEBEC.

READ BEFORE THE

Literary and Historical Society,

Quebec, 10th March, 1891,

BY

FRED. C. WÜRTELE, ESQ.

In writing the history of the Cathedral of the Holy
Trinity of Quebec, it will not be out of place to give a short
sketch of those good Monks and Friars of the order of St.
Francis who were the former proprietors of the land on
which the sacred edifice has been built.

The mendicant order of Monks, called Franciscans, was
founded in ~~Spain~~, in the year 1208, by St. Francis d'Assisi.*
Subsequently they spread into ~~Italy~~ and were introduced
into France by St. Louis of Gonzaga. They were also
called " Récollets," from the latin word " Recollectus," sig-
nifying " meditation " and also " gathering."

Their chief works were teaching, nursing the sick, and
ministering to the poor, whose wants they supplied out of
the donations and alms which they received. In fact their
livelihood was obtained entirely by begging, performed by
the " Frères Mineurs," and so highly were they esteemed
and beloved in old Canada, that the " habitants " would
always transport free of charge the results of their begging
expeditions from village to village and finally to the convent in Quebec. The boatmen invariably were pleased to
ferry them free across the St. Lawrence.

* DeSalignac.

Samuel de Champlain relates, that " he was convinced of " the necessity of religious instruction to influence such of " the Indian population of Canada as might be induced to " turn to agricultural pursuits." In this connexion he was directed by Sieur Louis Houel, at Brouage to apply to the General of the Order of Recollets. On the 10th October, 1614, at a meeting of the States General, held at Sens, where many Cardinals and Bishops were present, Champlain made his appeal ; the proposal was favorably received and money was subscribed towards the outfit of the Fathers. Four Recollets were chosen as missionaries to Canada, namely : Fathers Denis Jamay, the superior, Jean D'Olbeau, Joseph LeCaron and brother Pacifique Duplessis. They assembled at Rouen in March, 1615, and sailed from Honfleur on the 24th April, arriving at Tadousac on the 25th May and proceeded thence to Quebec. A temporary chapel and house were erected near the " Abitation," now the site of the Church of Notre-Dame des Victoires. Père D'Olbeau remained in Quebec and the three others went to Three Rivers to begin their work among the Indians.

In 1623 two more of the Order arrived, Père Nicolas Viel and Frère Gabriel Sagard, the first historian of Canada. So well did the Recollets master the Indian language that they compiled a grammar and dictionary of the Huron and Algonquin tongues, which the Jesuits subsequently found extremely useful, but did not give the originators much credit therefor.

As they had full permission both from Pope Paul V, and Louis XIII, of France, to own property in Canada, they chose a site near a river called by the Indians Cabirecoubat, and Saint Croix by Jacques Cartier, but to make a *souvenir* of their benefactor M. Charles de Boues, grand Vicaire de Pontoise, they named the river St. Charles. On its banks they began, on 7th September, 1619, to prepare building materials for a church, convent and seminary, and the corner stone was laid 3rd June, 1620, by Père D'Olbeau.

This was the first church erected in the French possessions in North America. The convent was first completed
but the church was not ready for consecration until 25th
May, 1621, and was named Notre-Dame des Anges. Père
LeClerq narrates that they still retained the house and chapel
erected in 1615, in the Lower Town of Quebec, and used them
as Hospice and " Chapelle succursale."

The establishment on the St. Charles was strongly built
and of a semi-military character, fitted with bastions and
surrounded with palissades, in order to guard against the
raids of the Indians. In fact the building was hardly completed when the Monks repulsed a serious attack of the
Iroquois.

The mission field was found to be so large that the Fathers, though advised to the contrary by their friends,
invited the Jesuits to assist them. This invitation was
heartily responded to, for on 19th June, 1625, several Jesuits
arrived at Quebec, but the authorities refused them permission to land. However, by the intercession of the
Recollets, leave was granted and the Jesuits were hospitably
entertained at the convent of Notre-Dame. They lived
there until their residence was completed at Hare Point, in
1627.

On 19th June, 1629, the brothers Kirke captured Quebec
and both Recollets and Jesuits were shipped back to France.
By the treaty of St. Germain, 29th March, 1632, Canada was
restored to France, and on 13th July of that year the French
flag again waved over Quebec.

The Jesuits returned to Canada but the Recollets were
refused permission to proceed there, the reason alleged was
that, as they were of a mendicant order of Monks, they were
unsuitable for that country; this opposition it seems was
inspired by the Jesuits.

However, in 1669, after repeated petitions and by the
intercession of M. Talon, the Intendant, permission was
granted and several Recollet Fathers sailed from Rochelle

for Canada with him. But they were unfortunately wrecked near Lisbon and returned to France whence they sailed the next year, arriving at Quebec with M. Talon, 18th August, 1670.

They resumed possession of their properties but found the buildings very dilapidated and almost in ruins. Nothing daunted, reconstruction was begun on 22nd June, 1671, and and the church was consecrated in 1673.

The governor, Frontenac, in 1677, built for them at his own expense a large convent, and in 1678 a chapel and sacristy were added, so that the property of Notre-Dame des Anges was put in better order than when they left Canada fifty years before. It is now the General Hospital.

The Recollets had not been ten years in possession of their convent when they wished to establish themselves in the Upper Town of Quebec, and on the * 8th May, 1681, they obtained from the King an emplacement called the "Senechaussée" or "Senechal's Jurisdiction," between Garden, St. Anne and St. Louis streets, on which they built by degrees a convent and church, but much against the wishes of the bishop, Monseigneur de Laval.

When Bishop St. Vallier was in Paris in March, 1692, he obtained from Louis XIV, a confirmation of the permission to the Franciscans, to be established in Canada. At the same time he obtained from the Father Provincial of the Recollets permission to negociate for the purchase of the property of Notre-Dame des Anges, which he required for the General Hospital. On the 15th August, 1692, Bishop St. Vallier arrived in Quebec with a reinforcement of fourteen Recollets.

On 13th September the transfer of the whole of the property on the St. Charles was made to the Bishop, containing six arpents, together with the Church and convent for the sum of 16,000 livres (about $3,600) cash down and 1,600

---

* 28th by Larcau, but 8th by the Jugement du Conseil Souverain.

livres ($360) per annum for five years. Also 2,000 livres ($450) for certain moveables. He also ceded them a small lot of ground one arpent in extent adjoining the property in Upper Town, at the end of Place d'Armes, opposite the Chateau St. Louis, with the buildings thereon then used as an hospital, which he had obtained from Sieur de la Durantaye. As they wished to reserve four arpents on the St. Charles for a garden and hermitage, St. Vallier preferred to give them a further sum of 1200 livres ($270) to enable them to purchase a site on the water side on which they built a chapel, the present " Chapelle de St. Roch." He also permitted the installation of their convent in Upper Town and promised them an annual charity of 50 crowns, and gave them the right to march in procession once a year to the General Hospital of Notre-Dame des Anges, there to celebrate grand mass.

At the siege of Quebec in 1759, the Recollet buildings were considerably damaged by the fire of the British, and the fall of Quebec was equally disastrous to the Recollets and Jesuits.

We find that in the capitulations signed at Montreal, 8th September, 1760, Article 32 contains as follows, and was " granted ".:—" The communities of nuns shall be preserved " in their constitutions and priviledges, they shall continue " to observe their rules: they shall be exempted from " lodging any military: and it shall be forbid to molest them " in their religious exercises, or to enter their monasteries: " safe guards shall ever be given them, if they desire them."

But Article 33 was " refused till the King's pleasure be known " it reads thus :—" The preceding article shall like-" wise be executed with regard to the communities of " Jesuits and Recollets, and of the house of the Priests of " St. Sulpice, at Montreal : these last, and the Jesuits shall " preserve their right to nominate to certain curacies and " missions as heretofore."

Monsieur Gravé, priest of the Seminary, in a letter to

Monsieur de Villars in Paris, on 25th October, 1763, tersely put it :—" Les Jésuites et les Récollets mourront chez eux, " mais n'auront point de successeurs," which the Recollets found too true.

Free passage was given in His Majesty's ships to those of the above orders who wished to leave the country and no doubt many availed themselves of this opportunity.

The number of Recollets diminished year by year, so that their convent was too large for them, but in 1776 we find that the unoccupied portion was used as a jail for political offenders, and the American prisoners taken in Montgomery's fatal attack on Quebec, 31st December of that year, were locked up there. Judge Henry in his memoirs graphically relates his incarceration there when taken prisoner on that memorable night. Subsequently the political prisoners DuCalvet, LaTerrière and others found the restraint imposed on them in the Recollet convent not very formidable, and were well cared for by the Monks.

The Recollets, all honor to them, were most liberal towards other religious denominations, for it is recorded in the *Quebec Gazette* of Thursday, 21st May, 1767, that :—" On " Sunday next, Divine service, according to the use of the " Church of England, will be at the Recollet's Church and " continue for the summer season, beginning soon after " eleven. The drum will beat each Sunday soon after half " an hour past ten, and the Recollet's bell will ring, to give " notice of the English service, the instant their own is " ended."

Again in the *Quebec Gazette* of 13th August, 1789, it is narrated how that on Wednesday, the 5th August, the Rt. Revd. Dr. Charles Inglis, * Bishop of Nova Scotia, held

* Dr. Charles Inglis was elected rector of Trinity parish New York, on the 20th March, 1777. His induction did not take place in one of the chapels, but he was brought to the ruins of the church (destroyed by fire on 21st Sept., 1776,) and inducted by placing his hand on the ruined wall. He resigned the rectorship on 1st November, 1783, and proceeded to Halifax in Nova Scotia. He was consecrated Bishop of Nova Scotia, on 12th October, 1787, being the first colonial Bishop of the Church of England. (Centennial history of the diocese of New York.)

arrived Halifax

his primary visitation in the Recollet's Church and the sermon was preached by the Revd. Philip Toosey, minister of the parish.

This same privilege was cheerfully accorded to the Presbyterians in Montreal in 1791, and it is stated † that the Treasurer of the Presbyterian congregation was directed to pay for a hogshead of wine given to the Recollets for using their Church. Also in 1809 † when the Presbyterian Church of Montreal was being repaired, service was again held in the Recollet's Church and it is stated :—" That the Recollet " Fathers politely refused any remuneration, but were in- " duced to accept a present of two hogsheads of Spanish " wine, containing some 60 gallons each, and a box of " candles in acknowledgment of their good offices, and that " they were thankful for the same."

On Tuesday, 11th August, 1789, a farewell address was presented to the Bishop of Nova Scotia, by the clergy of the Church of England of Quebec, (likely Canada,) signed by the Revds. David Francis DeMontmollin, Philip Toosey, D. Ch. Delisle, John Doty, John Stuart, James Tunstall, John Langhorn, L. J. B. N. Veysière.

The Bishop sailed for Halifax on the 17th, on board H. M. S. "Weazle," when a salute was fired in his honor.

It was reported in the *Quebec Gazette* of 19th September, 1793, that the British Government purposed turning out the Recollets and converting their Convent and Church into an English Protestant Church, but this was justly contradicted in the issue of the 26th, for the British Government would certainly never have treated with harshness those good Fathers who had been ever ready to grant the use of their churches to their Protestant brethren in Quebec and Montreal. Therefore I give the paragraphs as they appeared in the *Gazette* :—

19th September, 1793 :—" We hear that the Reverend " Père de Berrey, only surviving Père of the order of the

† Gregg's history of the Presbyterian Church in Canada.

" Recollets in Quebec, is to give up the Church and Convent
" of the order to be converted into an English Church and
" residence for the Protestant Bishop. Government will of
" course allow him a handsome annuity during life."

26th September, 1793:—To the Printer—" Sir,—You are
" requested to insert in your next *Gazette* that the public
" may be perfectly informed and disabused ; and the ano-
" nymous author of the paragraph inserted in the *Gazette*
" of the 19th instant, if he is not a fallacious and mischievous
" impostor, has made at least too great a mistake to expose
" it so publickly. To his false allegation it is answered that
" the Reverend Père de Berrey is by no means the only sur-
" viving Père of the order of the Recollets, and that several
" others are still adjoined to him, without the consent of
" whom, he cannot by himself, for any motive, give up the
" Church and Convent of his order ; and that he is not at all
" inclined to make such a cession ; the beneficence and
" disinterestment that he has constantly showed to this day
" towards the Protestant people, in permitting them, and
" even facilitating the exercise of their religion in his own
" Church, is a very authentic proof of his attentive zeal in
" obliging every one in the diversity of their sentiments.
" After this striking instance, how could it be said that,
" against the law of nations, he may be and his consorts
" spoliated of their property; and that a nation whose ur-
" banity, sentiments of honor and humanity form the
" character, can tell to the Proprietors : *Hæc mea sunt veteres*
" *migrate coloni.*"

The venerable Father was evidently in receipt of some
annuity or gratuity, for Mr. P. A. DeGaspé relates in his
memoirs that, " Père de Berrey, the superior of the order,
" received from the English Government a ' *Traitement* ' or
" recompense of 500 louis, equivalent to £1,500 of present
" money. Also that he had separate apartments in the
" Convent where he received his friends and gave dinners to

" the Governors, and also had the Duke of Kent as a frequent
" visitor."

The Recollet Convent and Church were burnt on the
afternoon of 6th September, 1796, and the disaster is thus
described in the *Quebec Gazette* of 8th September:—

" On Tuesday last, about four o'clock in the afternoon, a
" dreadful fire broke out in a stable belonging to the Hon-
" orable Thomas Dunn, in St. Louis street, which seemed
" for some time to threaten destruction to the greater part
" of the town. The wind blowing from the west instantly
" communicated the flames to the house of the Honorable
" Chief Justice Monk,* and to that adjoining on the east
" side. While these were burning with great violence and
" it was feared would communicate the flames to the adja-
" cent houses on both sides of the street, the fire was ob-
" served to have caught in the Convent of the Recollets, at
" the lower end of the street, at least two hundred yards
" from where it began. In a few minutes the roof and
" spire of the Church fell down, and the whole Convent was
" in a blaze. At that moment it seemed very doubtful
" whether the Castle or even the Lower Town could be
" saved; but the wind shifting a little to the northwards
" carried the flames up Carrières street, facing the Chateau
" garden, where the fire continued to rage, burning down
" all before it, until it reached the corner of the back street,
" which leads up towards Mount Carmel, where at last it
" stopped. Thirteen or fourteen houses in all were entirely
" burnt down."

This calamity rendered homeless the few monks that remained and they dispersed. Father de Berrey, the superior,
found a home with Mr. François Duval, in St. Louis street.
Frère Marc settled at St. Thomas and earned his living for
forty years by repairing clocks. Frère Louis François Mar
tinet dit Bonamie, § opened a school in St. Valier street and

---

* This is the site of the old Officers' quarters, now the residences of the Pay-
master Lieut. Col. Forrest and Brigade Major Taschereau, of the 7th Military
District.

§ Quebec Past and Present, by J. M. LeMoine.

had a good garden renowned for its flowers and fruits : he died at the age of eighty-three and was buried in St. Rochs, 12th August, 1848.

After the fire the Government * took possession of the property and razed the ruins. Part of the foundation wall, could till lately, be seen in the roadway between the Cathedral and Place D'Armes near the crossing. That portion of it now surrounded by a stone wall, forms the English Cathedral " Close."

In 1804 the Court House was built on another portion facing St. Louis street and Place D'Armes. .

After the burning of the Recollet Church, the services of the Church of England were held in the Jesuit's Church situate about the corner of St. Anne and Garden streets.

This Church † was demolished in 1807, as the ground was required on which to build the old Market Hall, since removed.

Thus ends the story of the Recollets in Quebec. ‡

To correct an error of nomenclature, in this paper, relative to the word "Monk" as applied to the order of St. Francis, it may be here stated that the Franciscans are not Monks, but a mendicant order of Friars, and the " Récollets " or " Frères Mineurs " are a branch or reform of that order established in 1532.

---

* The property of the Recollets was taken possession of shortly after the conquest, 1759, but the survivors were allowed to enjoy the usufruct until the death of the last of them, who was Father de Berrey. On his death in 1800, the property, which was not extensive, reverted to the Crown. (D. Brymner, Dominion Archivist.)

† A handsome marble slab stood near the door of the Governor's entrance, and when the church was demolished, the Governor presented this slab to the Lord Bishop of Quebec. It now forms the top of the Communion table of St. Paul's Church. [Correspondence relating thereto is in the Archives of the Diocese.]

‡ The Franciscans returned to Canada in 1890, and the Rev. Père Othon, the Provincial Superior, opened a convent in Richmond Street, in Montreal which was inaugurated in June by Archbishop Fabre.

The Protestant population in Canada had greatly increased, so much so that in 1791 provision was made by the King for the maintenance of the clergy of the Church of England, then the established Church in Canada, by means of a reservation of one-seventh of all the lands at the disposal of the Crown, which was called the "Clergy Reserves." That same year Canada was divided into the two provinces called Upper and Lower, the former being almost entirely Protestant. In 1793 the King decided to erect these provinces into a diocese to be called the Bishopric of Quebec, the Letters Patent of which were issued dated 28th June, 1793, and on the recommendation of the Bishop of Lincoln, the Archbishop of Canterbury appointed Dr. Jacob Mountain Lord Bishop of Quebec. This is the first time that the title of Lord Bishop was conferred upon a colonial bishop.

That year there were but nine Church of England clergymen in the two provinces, viz : six in the Lower and three in the Upper, five of whom were missionaries of the "Society for Propagation of the Gospel in Foreign Parts," and the remaining four were paid by Government. The churchmen of Quebec and Montreal were ministered to by two clergymen in each town, but the arrival of the Bishop put new life and energy into the Church.

Dr. Jacob Mountain was of Huguenot descent, his family having escaped to England at the revocation of the edict of Nantes, and settled in Norfolk. He was born in 1750, and at one time was rector of St. Andrew's Church in Norwich ; afterwards he removed to Buckden, in Huntingdonshire, of which place he was Vicar and also examining chaplain to the Bishop of Lincoln who resided there. He was consecrated at Lambeth, 7th July, 1793, and immediately took ship for his diocese and arrived at Quebec on the 1st November, after a voyage of thirteen weeks, and proceeded to the residence appointed for him at Woodfield, on the St. Louis road, where he lived till 1802.

As coming to Canada in those days was deemed complete

exile, besides his wife and four children, he was accompanied by his sister-in-law, two sisters, his elder brother, *
Dr. Jehoshaphat Mountain, rector of Peldon, in Essex, with
his wife, two daughters and his son, the Rev. Salter Jehoshaphat Mountain, M.A., who was the bishop's chaplain.
Thirteen Mountains in all. Thus the diocese was at once
increased by two clergymen besides the Bishop, but there
was no building in Quebec belonging to the Church of
England in which to conduct the services of the Church.

The retired Roman Catholic Bishop Briand, the "ancien
Evêque de Québec," then an infirm but venerable old man,
upon being introduced to the Protestant Bishop, appeared
unfeignedly rejoiced at his arrival and greeting him with
the antiquated salutation of a kiss upon each cheek, declared that—"it was high time for such a measure, to keep
your people in order."

It was necessary that the diocese should have a coat of
arms to be used as the seal of the diocese, and for other
necessary purposes, therefore the King commanded, by his
warrant dated 16th July, 1793, Charles Duke of Norfolk,
Earl Marshal of England, who ordered Sir Isaac Heard,
Garter King of arms, to devise the armorial ensign, which
was patented on the 8th August and described as follows :—

‡ "Perfess wavy azure and gules in chief, a book open
" proper clasped and ornamented gold ; upon the book a
" crozier in bend or ; in base a lion passant-gardant of the
" fourth, holding in the dexter paw a key erect argent ; in
" a canton of the last a cross of the second between four
" corners patée-fitchée sable. The book is an emblem of
" the gospel. The crozier of the consecrated character of
" the Bishop of the See. The lion of England in the base
" supporting a key, indicates the sacred confidence reposed
" by the Sovereign as supreme head of the Church, in the

* Dr. Mountain was minister at Montreal in 1813.

‡ In the Archives of the Diocese.

" Bishop, and the undulated line is a symbol of the transat-
" lantic situation of the See. The cross of St. George in the
" canton marks the delegation from the sovereignty of Eng-
" land, and the four corners patée-fitchée, being the part of
" the arms of the See of Canterbury, point out the subordina-
" tion of the Bishop of Quebec, as a suffragan to the Archi-
" episcopal See." This coat of arms is to be seen over the
Bishop's throne in the Cathedral.

In 1797 the Rev. Philip Toosey, curate of Quebec, died
and the Government appointed the Rev. Salter Jehoshaphat
Mountain the Bishop's chaplain, to succeed him, by letters
patent of 15th September.

As previously stated, the services of the Church of England
were held in the Recollet Church and afterwards in the
Jesuits' Chapel, but in 1799, at the solicitation of the Bishop,
King George III, at his own expense, proceeded to build a
Church in Quebec and for that purpose set apart a portion
of the Recollet property, bounded by the parade ground,
St. Anne and Garden streets, with the proviso that no other
building whatsoever be permitted within the " Close" other
than the Cathedral, under penalty of forfeiture of the whole
property to the Crown.* Letters patent were issued on 11th
November, appointing a commission consisting of the Lord
Bishop, William Osgoode, Chief Justice of Lower Canada,
Sir George Pownall, Kt., the Rev. Salter J. Mountain, rector
of the parish, and Jonathan Sewell, the Attorney General,
for the purpose of erecting a " Metropolitan Church " in the
city of Quebec. Plans and specifications were at once prepared and Captain Robe, of the Royal Artillery, was appointed superintendent of the work, for which services he
received £300. Matthew Bell, Esq., was treasurer of the
commission. The necessary funds were paid from time to
time on estimates furnished by the commission in sums of
£300, and the greatest economy was enjoined by the Pro-

* Appendix A. (In the archives of the Cathedral.)

vincial Secretary, Herman Witsius Ryland. The money
came through the Commissariat Department. The first
stone was laid 11th August, 1800, and the corner stone was
laid by His Excellency the Lieutenant-Governor, and the
following document placed therein :—

Glory to God in the Highest !

" Of this Metropolitan Church of Quebec, erected by the
pious munificence of His Majesty George III, King of Great
Britain, France and Ireland, the first stone was laid by His
Excellency R. S. Milnes, Lieutenant-Governor of this Province, assisted by the Rev. Jacob, Lord Bishop of this
diocese, the Hon. Wm. Osgoode, His Majesty's Chief Justice
for the Province, the Hon. Sir George Pownall, Kt., member
of the Legislative Council, Jonathan Sewell, Esq., Attorney
General, and the Rev. Salter J. Mountain, Rector of Quebec,
Commissioners for building the Church, and Matthew Bell,
Esq., their Treasurer, on the 3rd day of November, in the
year of Our Lord one thousand eight hundred, and the
forty-first year of His Majesty's reign."

This grand old Cathedral is a plain but substantial rec-
tangular edifice, standing in the centre of a well kept
"Close," and surrounded by a low stone wall, which is
surmounted on the street sides with an iron railing ; * all
along this wall stand those fine old trees, † adding beauty
to the environment and reminding Englishmen of these
sacred buildings in Britain, one of which it closely resem-
bles. Two large and two small iron gates form the entrances
from the " Parade ground," now called the Place d'Armes,
but the main entrance is on Garden street, with a small
gate on either side of the large one, over which is a lamp.
Let us pass through the main gate, ascend the stone steps
which extend along the whole front of the building, the

* Railing was made by Mr. Henry Blackburn.

† The elms are older than the Church, but the bass wood trees were planted
by Thos. May, Esq., in 1826.

top one forming a broad platform, and enter by the centre door. In the vestibule, over the inner door, is a grey stone slab, the legend thereon relates : —

The first stone laid
August 11, 1800.
This stone, the last
laid May 1st, 1804 by
Ed. Cannon, Mar. Man. — (master mason.)

The architectural description and dimensions cannot be more accurately described than in Captain Robe's own words :—

	ft.	in.		ft.	in.
Extreme length	134	9	Breadth of windows	5	0
Length of foundation of tower..	21	7	Height of "	5	6
Breadth " " ..	21	0	Height of upper windows	11	0
Length between cross walls	89	0	Length of pews	7	6
Breadth of Altar	36	0	Breadth of "	3	0
Depth "	18	0	Breadth of middle aisle	10	0
Extreme breadth of building	73	0	" of side aisles	4	0
Breadth within	65	0	Vestry rooms square	14	0
Distance between centres of columns	16	3	Height from plinth outside to top of stone cornices	36	6
Breadth of gallery	13	0	Height of steeple above cornice	114	0
Staircase rooms { length	16	0			
{ breadth	14	0			

The general dimensions of this Church were in great measure taken from those of the Church of St. Martin's, in the Fields, London, but the state of materials and workmanship in Canada made a plain design necessary.

The east and west ends are ornamented with pilasters of the Ionic according to Palladio and supporting a modillion cornice and pediment but without a frieze ; this idea was taken from the Pantheon at Rome so executed, and was done to give more boldness to the pilasters for the intended height of the building. The pilasters project less than Palladio's rule directs, owing to the Pointe-aux-Trembles stone, which, in the then state of the quarries could not be got in masses large enough without an enormous expense. The pediments are surmounted with oblate vases which at the angles of the building serve as flues for the stoves within the Church.

Owing also to the smallness of the material, the stones of the cornices are much cramped with iron within the wall.

The tower is sixteen feet square within, and contains space for eight bells, and above the stone work is a cupola and spire of wood covered with tin whose whole height from the ground is 154 feet.

The general plan of the Church was given by Captain Hall, of the Royal Artillery, the detailed plans of the several parts were drawn by myself.

The designs within the Church are all my own, as well as the construction of the roof, although throughout the work I had continually the aid of Capt. Hall's judgment and good taste.

The roof and galleries are connected with the pillars by strong screw bolts and iron straps and let well into the walls.

The proportions of the main columns and entablatures are from Palladio, as correctly followed as wood work would admit.

The whole designs within the Church are of the ancient Ionic order, but from the proportions of different approved masters according to their situation.

The galleries with the pillars under the organ are from Alberti's proportions, the volutes formed in his manner, and the only deviation from him is the dentel added to the cornice, Alberti giving two plain faciæ.

The throne is a continuation of the same design but having its columns fluted and its volutes with a third turn.

The cornices in the small rooms are from the same masters, but without the dentel.

The east window is the Ionic of Vitruvius according to Vignola, the shafts having a small addition of length to suit the opening.

The pulpit is the Ionic of Alberti, the design of it and the reading desks are my own.

The pillars supporting the stairs behind the pulpit are

taken from some peculiarly plain Pillars in the Coliseum at Rome. The organ is a design of my own and is yet incomplete, the base of the large case is moulded from the Ionic of Vitruvius, and the capitals intended for it are from an open network design in the temple of Erecthia at Athens and described in Blondel's works, now in the Quebec Library. The temporary caps on the Choir organ are gilt with scroll ornaments from the same.

The real design is for carved work of the colour of the wood only, with wreaths of oak leaves down the panels, and a drapery to cover the tops of the pipes.

The fretwork of the arch is my own, and is in imitation of the ancient stucco work, the idea was taken from the common mode of ceiling rooms in Quebec with board and batten, which I thought, if crossed diagonally might have a good effect.

It only remains to give the names of the workmen who distinguished themselves.

MASONS.

Edward Cannon, master,
Ambrose, ⎫
Lawrence, ⎬ his sons.
John,* ⎭

⎧ Mr. Cannon with his sons
⎪ laid almost all the cut stone,
⎨ a considerable part of which
⎪ was cut by them and also part
⎩ of the ornamented stone work.

Henry Deas, an excellent workman, cut most part of the bases and of the wreaths round the openings of the pediments.

---

* The only survivor of the family of John Cannon is James Cannon, Esq., Advocate, and Deputy Marshal of the Vice-Admiralty Court, at the city of Quebec.

The other children were :—

Mrs. Eleanore Cannon, wife of Denis Murray, Esq., and mother of Denis Murray, Esq., Judge of the Sessions of the Peace.

The Rev. John Francis Cannon, Parish Priest of Cornwall, Ontario ; died April, 1854.

Edward George Cannon, Esq., Notary Public ; resided for many years and up to the time of his death at No. 6 Donnacona street ; died 13th October, 1885.

And Lawrence Ambrose Cannon, Esq., Advocate, and City Clerk of Quebec ; died 3rd April, 1890.

John Bryson, a good workman, did some part of the same work.

Joseph Petitclerc, first began to cut stone in this employ and was able to cut some of the ornaments on the vases. These were the best masons.

PLASTERERS.

Joseph Whitcomb, an American, undertook this work, and with his brother and a man named Topping executed it.

CARPENTERS.

Jean Baptiste Bedard, the master carpenter, constructed all the carpenter's work in the columns, roof and steeple. The latter is peculiarly his trade and his work in that respect is expert. He was particularly assisted by two men of the name of Cardinal and one named Fortier.

JOINERS.

Henry Henderson, the master, an excellent workman.

Alex. Bryson, brother to the mason. Sam. Fox. { These two very capable workmen. They made the galleries principally.

Chas. Marié, a good workman. The winding stairs are his own work.

Pierre Roi, a good workman. The pulpit stairs were done by him.

John McKutcheon, a master joiner, but employed here by the day. His work is principally about the round work of the pulpit and the returns of the galleries. He turned the bases and capitals of the large columns.

Thos. Herring, a good workman; since dead.

These were the principal joiners; there were many others very capable, but inferior workmen.

PAINTER.

Paul Thibodo, a joiner, painted the ceiling except over the Altar.

PAINTER AND GILDER.

Wm. Cartwright, a capital workman. He painted the columns and the Altar and painted the Commandments.

He also gilt the front of the Organ. He was a discharged soldier from the 7th Regiment of Foot and afterwards enlisted in the New Brunswick Fencibles.

CARVER.

Thomas Fitzer, an ingenious mechanic, by trade a ladies' shoemaker from Birmingham. He first undertook the guilloche ornament between the columns and afterwards the capitals of the columns. He also set up the Organ and tuned it, and was employed for that purpose afterward.

TURNER.

P. LaFleur, turned the columns within the Church except the large columns.

TINMEN.

Colin Campbell made the vane and ball.

J. B. Valière covered the roof and steeple with tin.

SMITHS.

David Douglas made all the best smith's work.

WM. ROBE,

Major Royal Artillery, late Superintendent
for building the Cathedral Church.
Quebec, October 3rd, 1806.

The masons began laying the foundations 11th August, 1800. Service was performed in it 4th August, 1804.

List of books and papers sent herewith to Rev. Mr. Mountain for the Church:—

1 check book of the workmen employed.

5 small check books and 4 books of the joiners' time.

1 book of Estimates, 31st March, 1802.

1 book, copies of the Treasurer's accounts.

1 bundle of papers containing estimates, measurement, &c.

1 bundle of papers concerning the organ and bells.

3 plans, viz:—Of the foundation.

Of the ground and drains.

Of the inside shewing the design of the organ.   WM. ROBE.

The walls of the Cathedral are built of stone obtained from Ange-Gardien, Cap Rouge and Pointe-aux-Trembles. These different varieties having been found necessary for the several parts of the work.

The underflooring of the galleries is of pine, that of the Church is of cedar and all the upper flooring of oak. It is laid down in rebate, that is, half of the thickness of the edge on each side of the plank, is cut away to an equal depth and the flooring laid by overlapping these edges, the half cut or step from one being filled up by the half part left in the other, and fastened down with nails and pegs. The pillars are of pitch pine encased with other wood. The arched ceiling is entirely of pine, plaster having been deemed unsuitable for the climate. The height of the centre of the great arch from the floor is 41 feet and from the floor to the top of the entablature of the pillars 23 feet. The chancel is semicircular inside on a radius of 18 feet. On the wall within the chancel to the south side of the altar, are the " Ten Commandments," written on two large tablets having broad gilt cable borders, and completely fill the space between the pillars ; opposite these are two similar tablets containing the Lord's Prayer and Apostles' Creed. All the pews and communion railing are of oak ; this railing is in its original position, but the arrangements of the open space in front of it have been considerably altered. The ancient oaken pulpit placed in the centre was in form a twelve sided polygon, and was reached on either side by staircases entered from the front and meeting on a platform in rear. Directly in front and attached to the pulpit was the reading desk, with a door on each side, and in front of this the clerk's desk.

The Bishop's throne was situated on the south side facing the reading desk, with its side against the first pillar ; a small pew for the verger was placed at the end nearest the Vestry door. In front of the foremost pew and abutting against the throne was a pew for the Divinity students.

On the north side adjoining the first pillar and facing the reading desk was the pew for the clergy, and midway between these was a small irregular octagonal font of cut stone, placed on a wooden pedestal. This font and the old Royal Arms in front of the Governor General's pew are now in St. Paul's Church in Champlain street, (the Mariners' chapel.) The font now in use was brought from England in 1831, by the Revd. Dr. Mills. *

Three quaint looking stoves were imported from London, two of them are still in use at the upper end of the Church.

The pews under the galleries ended at the second pillar and the remaining space was filled up with benches. †

The centre aisle contained the twenty-one oaken seats, which are still in use. On either side of the centre door against the wall were six pews in three rows, leaving a passage seven feet wide between them and the two rows of pews of the centre aisle.

The Communion plate was the special gift of the King and consists of ~~twelve~~ *ten* massive pieces of solid silver, exquisitely engraved and embossed with the Royal Arms and the arms of the diocese. The alms dish is a particularly beautiful work of art, the bottom being a representation, in relief, of the Lord's supper. A large credence patin, two tall flagons, two heavy chalices of frosted silver, ~~two small plain chalices~~, two massive candlesticks, ~~one large alms plate~~, and two plain patins, with the following inscription engraved on them : *the large plate & one small chalice were given by the King through per. Murray 27 June 1766 were made by Thomas Heming London 1763 - the other chalice made in Quebec 1837 by L. Amiot*

* When in England, he was commissioned by Archdeacon Mountain, in a letter dated 3rd February, 1831, to purchase a handsome Font for the Cathedral, to the value of £20. It was moreover to be sufficiently large so that infants could be baptized in it by immersion, and to be in harmony with the character of the building and therefore not gothic. He was to bring it out with him, which he no doubt did, although its arrival is not recorded.

† This description is from a copy of the floor plan drawn from the original by Mr. J. T. Lewis, in February, 1829, and is in the Archives of the Church.

Hanc Pateram
Nec non Cœteram supellectilem argenteam
Divino cultui accomodatum
In usum
Ecclesiæ Consociatæ Angliæ et Hibernæ
In Diocesi Quebencensi fundatæ
Sacrari Voluit
Georgii Tertii Britanniarum Regis
Pia munificentia
Anno ab Incarnatione
MDCCCIV

This service, which is a masterpiece of silversmith workmanship, was manufactured by Rundell & Edge, of London, and attracted considerable attention when placed on view in their establishment before being despatched to Quebec.

The old pulpit hangings and altar cloths, fringed with gold bullion lace, together with the Bible and Prayer Books, were also the gifts of His Majesty.

The organ was composed of two separate instruments, the great, and in front of it a smaller one, called the choir organ. These were ordered on the 5th September, 1801, from Thomas Elliot, Artillery Place, London, at a cost of £369 11s. 10d. cy., subscribed as follows:—

			£	s.	d.	
H. Caldwell,	£50 stg.,	equal to	£55	11s.	1d.	cy.
Lord Bishop of Quebec,	50	"	55	11	1	"
Revd. Salter Mountain,	25	"	27	15	6½	"
Sir Geo. Pownall,	20	"	22	4	5	"
Jonathan Sewell,	25	"	27	15	6½	"
Collected by J. Gay,			168	11	2	"
Justice Williams.			10	0	0	"
M. Dénéchaud			2	2	0	"
			£369	11	10	"

The Church was ready for consecration * in 1804, when the letters patent giving the property over to the Bishop

---

* Sentence of Consecration in the Appendix B. Rough draft and certificate in the Archives of the Cathedral.

were executed, and towards the end of August, the Commissioners notified the Bishop that all was ready and petitioned him to perform that ceremony, which took place on the 28th August and is thus described in the *Quebec Gazette* of 6th September :

"On Tuesday, 28th August, was consecrated the new "Cathedral Church of the Diocese of Quebec. At the usual "time of Divine service, the Lord Bishop was received at "the west door, by the commissioners appointed for erect-"ing the Church, by the clergy who were present, and "many respectable persons of the congregation assembled "for the purpose, and a petition presented to him praying "that he would consecrate the building, was read by the "secretary. His Lordship was from thence conducted to his "throne, by these gentlemen in procession, up the middle "aisle; on taking possession of which he addressed the "commissioners, to thank them, now that the building was "completed, for the zealous attention and important assist-"ance which they had given during the progress of the "work. A message was then sent to His Excellency the "Lieutenant Governor ; and immediately upon his entering "the Church, the hymn of ' God save the King ' with an "appropriate stanza was played upon the organ and sung ": by the choir. The Bishop and clergy then went to the "west door, and returned in the same order as before "towards the altar, repeating at the same time the 24th "Psalm, and after his Lordship had opened the service "peculiar to the occasion at the altar, the endowment of the "Church, and other instruments were then presented to "him, by the Hon. Sir George Pownall, knight, the Hon. "John Craigie, and Mr. Sewell, Attorney General, and the "former was read by the ' Official.' The Cathedral service "was now performed by the officiating clergy, and the "choir ; and was closed by an appropriate and excellent "discourse by the Revd. Dr. Mountain, Lord Bishop's "Official, from 1st Kings, 8 chapter, 27th verse. The

" whole was observed with the greatest good order and
" propriety and formed a truly interesting and impressive.
" scene ; every one appearing to join in the service with that
" devout earnestness which was naturally to be expected
" from the solemnity of the occasion, and from the comfort
" and blessing which they felt of being provided, through
" the bounty of our most gracious Sovereign, with a church
" in every respect suitable to the sacred character of a
" place appropriated to the performance of Divine Worship."

The organist was Dr. Bentley, who had a surpliced choir
of 13 boys and 4 men. The Revd. Mr. Fielde acted as pre-
centor, and the Cathedral was opened with a full choral
service, which it is said was regularly maintained as long
as a clergyman could be found to conduct it. The surpliced
choir was kept up for some forty years.

It is universally acknowledged that the acoustic qualities
of the Cathedral "par excellence," are unsurpassed.

The edifice cost $80,000.

When the Bishop was in England in 1808, he received a
visit from the Hon. and Revd. Charles James Stewart,
brother of the Earl of Galloway, who expressed a desire to
be employed in the diocese of Quebec. This offer was gladly
accepted and Mr. Stewart proceeded to Quebec and was
sent as a missionary to the borders of Lake Champlain,
taking charge of St. Armands on Missisquoi Bay, where he
was instrumental in the formation of new missions and the
erection of several Churches, thus giving fresh impulse to
religion and to the advancement of the established Church
in the Eastern townships. While on a visit to England Mr.
Stewart succeeded in raising a fund for building Churches
in Canada.

On the 16th January, 1814, the Bishop's son, George Jehoshaphat, was ordained priest and licensed as evening
lecturer at the Cathedral, but subsequently he received the
appointment of Rector of Fredericton, New Brunswick, as
well as Chaplain to the Legislative Council and also to the

garrison; he arrived there on the 27th September of that year. On the Revd. Salter Mountain removing in 1816, to Cornwall, in Upper Canada, the Revd. George returned to Quebec.

The Bishop, who was at this time visiting in England, prevailed on the Government to institute the office of "Commissary" or "Official" for both Upper and Lower Canada. His son having been nominated to that of Lower Canada, in a measure somewhat relieved his Lordship of some of the necessary but arduous visitations through this extensive diocese. These journeys, besides being attended with a great deal of hardship and some danger when travelling in canoes, took up too much valuable time in slow transit from place to place.

The parish of Quebec had been erected and defined in a certain " Règlement " of Sieur de Vandreuil, Governor of New France, the Bishop and Intendant Begon, on the 20th September, 1721, which deed was confirmed by an " Arrêt " of the King of France in Conseil d'Etat, dated 3rd March, 1722. Lord Dalhousie adopted these same limits of this ecclesiastical division, calling it the Parish of Quebec in the diocese of Quebec, in his Letters Patent * issued in the name of King George IV, dated 8th September, 1821, whereby the Revd. George Jehoshaphat Mountain was inducted Rector of Quebec, and " declaring that, as there is at pre-" sent no parish Church, appartaining to the Church of " England in the parish of Quebec, the Cathedral be used as, " and applied to the purposes of a parochial or parish " Church of the parsonage or rectory and parish of Quebec, " reserving to the Bishop and his successors all rights, pri-" vileges, &c., belonging to him and them in respect to the " said Cathedral Church and provided always that the Cathe-" dral shall be used as a parish Church only until a parish " Church shall be built in the said parish of Quebec."

* In the Archives of the Cathedral.

As there was no rectory or parsonage house, the Governor in Council endowed the rectory with a piece of land on which to build a parsonage house and premises as a freehold and inheritance vested in the Rector of the Parish Church of Quebec, " who will have and enjoy all rights, " emoluments, &c., &c., thereunto belonging, in the same " manner, terms and conditions and liable to the perform- " ance of the same duties as the incumbent of a Rectory in " England."

The land granted for this purpose is that adjoining the Cathedral Close, and is described as beginning on the southeast side of Garden street, " thence along the new wall " separating this ground from that belonging to the Cathe- " dral Church, south 77° east magnetically, 161 feet ; thence " at right angles or south 13° west 60 feet taking in 5½ feet " of the cistern, thence south 74° west 77 feet to the gable " end of the house on Mr. Fraser's property, thence along " the same north, 19° 30' west 40 feet, thence along the " north-east boundary of Mr. Fraser's property, south 82° " 30' west 81 feet, to Garden street, thence along the same " north 17° 30' east 97 feet to the place of beginning, con- " taining 12694 superficial English feet."

The Government, by Letters Patent * of 9th January, 1820, established two archdeaconries in the diocese, that in Upper Canada, called York, to which the Revd. George O'Kill Stewart was named, and Dr. George Jehoshaphat Mountain was appointed Archdeacon of Quebec.

The Quebec Sunday School was established in April, 1823, in connection with the diocesan committee of the Society for Promoting Christian Knowledge, and was opened in the old Hope Gate Guard-House, in the rooms occupied by the National Schools opened there in 1819, and when the National Schools removed to their new building † near

---

* In the Archives of the Diocese.
† Copy of Patent of this lot is in the Archives of the Diocese.

St. John's Gate, the Sunday School moved there also. Those attending it were from the National and Garrison Schools and also many other children of the parish ; and as it was conducted by the Archdeacon, assisted by the Revd. George Archbold and the ladies and gentlemen who kindly volun-teered their services as teachers were altogether members of the Cathedral ; this is the foundation of the Cathedral Sunday School.

At the St. John street burying ground was the Sexton's house in which a room had been set apart for the perform-ance of the burial service, and in 1822, the Archdeacon used to hold service in it for the Jersey and Guernsey people and others who wished to attend. This room soon became too small and the whole house was then converted into a chapel and the Sexton transferred to other quarters. This is the origin of St. Matthew's Church.

The Bishop now advanced in years, wished to retire from active work, and when the Archdeacon was in England in 1825, he tried to arrange for his father's retirement, but the Government would not hear of such a thing. Even while these negociations were proceeding, and during his son's absence, the venerable Prelate and devoted servant of God was passing away forever to be at rest from his labors, dying at his residence, Marchmont, on the 16th June, 1825, at the age of 76. During the thirty-two years he presided over the See of Quebec, the Church had greatly increased throughout Canada, many missions were established in remote parts and churches built ; he began his labors with only nine clergymen to assist him, but at his death there were sixty-one ministers and two archdeacons in the diocese, with a corporation of the clergy in both Upper and Lower Canada for the management of the Clergy Reserves. He lies buried within the Communion rails of the Cathedral, at the foot of that fine monument erected to his memory.

The obituary notice appeared in the *Quebec Gazette* of the 18th June, as follows :

DIED.—At Marchmont, near this city, on Thursday last, (16th), in the 76th year of his age, after a lingering illness, The Right Reverend Jacob Mountain, D.D., Lord Bishop of Quebec. His Lordship's mortal remains were conveyed this day at 8 o'clock from the Castle of St. Louis, to the Protestant Cathedral, and deposited in the vault of the Church. His Lordship was the first Bishop of this diocese, to which he was consecrated in the year 1793.

The following notice has been circulated on this melancholy occasion :

" CASTLE OF ST. LOUIS,

Saturday, June 13th, 1825."

" With sentiments of the deepest concern, the Lieutenant Governor notifies to the public the demise, on the night of Thursday last, of the Right Reverend the Lord Bishop of Quebec. In adverting to the unaffected piety, extended charity, and long residence in this province of the late Bishop, the Lieutenant Governor conceives he only anticipates the unanimous feeling of this community, when he announces his desire that every practicable degree of respect and veneration should be manifested on this most distressing occasion, to the memory of this excellent and lamented Prelate."

By order of His Excellency the Lieutenant Governor,

" LOUIS MONTIZAMBERT,

Actg.-Civil Secty.

The following account of the funeral is taken from the *Quebec Gazette* of 23rd :—

" On Monday (20th June) afternoon, the remains of the
" late Venerable Bishop of this diocese were interred in the
" Cathedral Church. The body had been removed from his
" Lordship's late residence to the Old Castle, from whence
" the interment took place at three o'clock, when the corpse
" was brought out in a coffin covered with black cloth and

" ornamented with black furniture and placed upon the
" hearse. The procession then moved through a lane formed
" by the regiments in garrison, from the Castle to the west
" door of the Cathedral ; the fine bugles of the 71st Regi-
" ment playing the dead march in Saul, and the medical
" attendants of the deceased preceding the hearse, which
" was followed by His Excellency the Lieutenant Governor,
" the Chief Justice, the gentlemen of the two Councils, the
" Judges and members of the Bar, in their gowns, the mili-
" tary officers off duty, the gentlemen of the civil and
" military departments, and a long train of respectable
" citizens in deep mourning. On arriving at the Church
" yard, the body was received by the Reverend Clergy in
" their surplices, over which they wore black scarfs, and on
" entering the Church, the Reverend Dr. Mills (Military
" Chaplain), commenced the burial service, in the course of
" which two anthems were performed, the first composed
" by the late Dr. Beckwith, of Norwich, the second ' I heard
" a voice from heaven,' &c., was composed for the occasion
" by Mr. Codman, the scientific organist of the Cathedral.
" The first part of the service having been gone through in
" a most solemn and impressive manner, the body was re-
" moved from the centre aisle and deposited in a vault on
" the left side of the Communion Table, when the remainder
" of the service was read."

The Hon. and Revd. Dr. Charles James Stewart was
appointed Lord Bishop of Quebec, and was consecrated on
Sunday, 1st January, 1826, in the Archiepiscopal chapel, at
Lambeth Palace, by his grace the Archbishop of Canter-
bury, assisted by the Bishop of London, Landaff and others.
But the Government still refused to divide the diocese into
Quebec and Upper Canada. The Bishop was installed in
the Cathedral on Sunday, 4th June, 1826.

Chief Justice Jonathan Sewell built a "Chapel of ease "
to the Cathedral, on St. Stanislas street, named the Chapel of
the Holy Trinity. The corner stone was laid on the 16th

September, 1824, and the Chapel was opened for service on the 27th November, 1825, when his son, the Revd. Edmund Willoughby Sewell, was appointed incumbent.*

The Asylum for widows and orphans had been for some time established in premises on the Lorette or Little River Road, known as " La Maison Rouge," but it being found to be inconveniently situated, the property was now sold and the Asylum removed to town.

The Cathedral up to this time had no bells, when on the 23rd April, 1828, an appeal was made for subscriptions † to obtain them, and on the 15th of May, at a meeting of the Congregation, it was resolved to order a chime of eight bells from Thomas Mears, of London, which arrived in the spring fleet of 1830, and cost $2,800.

Tenor Bell 3 ft. 9½ in. diam. in Key of F., weighs 1852 ℔s.

No. 7.	—3 "	4½ "	"	G,	"	1253	"
6.	—3 "	2¼ "	"	A.	"	1127	"
5.	—2 "	11¼ "	"	Bb,	"	893	"
4.	—2 "	9½ "	"	C,	"	794	"
3.	—2 "	7¼ "	"	D,	"	744	"
2.	—2 "	6 "	"	E,	"	704	"
Treble	—2 "	5¼ "	"	F,	"	654	"

Total.............................8021 "

The bells were rung for the first time on Wednesday, 20th October, 1830, when Lord Aylmer took the oaths of office as Administrator of the Government of Lower Canada.

---

* Revd. E. W. Sewell was admitted to the Diaconate on 11th May, 1824, by the Bishop of Quebec, Dr. Jacob Mountain, and was ordained priest by his successor the Rt. Revd. Dr. Charles James Stewart, on the 27th December, 1827. He died at Quebec on 24th October, 1890, at the advanced age of 91 years.

† The subscription list was headed by His Excellency, Sir J. Kempt, with £50. The Bishop gave a like amount. Sir J. Sherbrooke, £77 stg., and the sum of £37 10s. was given jointly by William Patton, Jonathan Wurtele and C. F. Aylwin, Esquires, being their fee from the Court as Arbitrators in the case of Bishop vs. Hunter. The Ven. Archdeacon Mountain £20, and the rest of the required amount was raised among the parishioners.

The ceremony took place in the Castle St. Lewis, Sir James Kempt, the retiring Governor, being present, and the Cathedral bells rang out their first peal to the accompaniment of a salute fired from the Citadel as a welcome to his Lordship. The *Quebec Mercury* of the 26th October, thus relates how that :—" The bells of the English Cathedral were first " chimed on the occasion of Lord Aylmer taking the oaths " of office as Administrator of the Government. They have " been hung with great ingenuity in the belfry by Mr. " Cole, of St. John street, who is we understand an exper- " ienced campanulist, and is instructing some young men " of the city in the art of ringing. The tones of the Quebec " bells are particularly mellow ; although the ropes have " not yet been affixed, and they have been rung only by " hand, their full effect has not been ascertained. This is " the first peal of bells which has been hung in this country."

On 24th December, 1831, letters patent, * were issued by the Government, granting a portion of La Vacherie farm, opposite the Marine Hospital, bounded by Water, Stewart, Panet and Dorchester streets, containing 31,311 feet, French measure, to the Bishop and his successors, for the purpose of building a Church and a burying ground.

The temporal affairs of the Cathedral were hitherto man· aged by the Church-Wardens, but in 1832 it was found desirable that besides the wardens, a vestry of twelve gentle· men should be appointed annually by the Congregation, which election took place on 15th July, resulting in the first vestry being composed of Hon. A. W. Cochrane, John Greaves Clapham, Noah Freer, John Jones, jr., James Hunt, William Philips, Henry Trinder, Captain John Sewell, Henry J. Russell, J. Thirlwall, J. B. Forsyth and Henry Lemesurier, Esqs. The names of the vestry were directed to be placed at each entrance of the Church, and it was also

---

* Copy in the Archives of the Diocese.

decided " that the vestry do take up the collections in
" rotation at every Sunday service, two collectors down-
" stairs and one in each gallery, and that each one, after
" completing his collection, shall, without passing within
" the rails, deposit the plate upon the projecting ledge under
" the ' Commandments,' on one side, and under the ' Belief
" and Lord's Prayer,' on the other side within the chancel,
" and that two plated articles be obtained for taking up
" these collections as there were not sufficient plates for the
" purpose."

The Mariners' Chapel in Champlain street was built in
1831 and consecrated on 3rd June, 1832, and named St.
Paul's.

The Cathedral was closed from the 4th to 18th August,
1833, for alterations, consisting of the erection of additional
galleries at the west end of the Church, on each side of the
organ, designed to accommodate the persons who sat on
benches under the north and south galleries, and the space
occupied by these benches was pewed, and all the pews in
the Church were numbered.

In April, 1834, St. Peter's Chapel, combined with the
Male Orphan Asylum, was opened in a stone house purchased from Mr. George Pozer, in "Rue de l'Eglise," St. Rochs.

Bishop Mountain, on his return from England in 1837,
brought with him the Rev. George Mackie, of Pembroke
College, Cambridge, to be his examining chaplain and to
assist him in the parish of Quebec, subsequently he named
him his " official." He also wished to have him appointed
rector of Quebec, but the Government would only do so by
the sacrifice of the rector's salary, which was not thought
advisable in the existing circumstances of the Church, so
the Bishop remained Rector of Quebec. Through the exertions of the Bishop and the Rev. G. Mackie, a religious
library was formed for the Congregations of the Cathedral
and the Chapel of the Holy Trinity ; the books, numbering

about 100 volumes, were kept in the north-east vestry of the Cathedral.

The continual accession to the Protestant population of Canada caused the episcopal labors to increase to such an extent as to make the Bishop feel more strongly than ever, and especially as his health was rapidly declining, that same want of assistance which had been experienced by his predecessor, and he determined to provide for it by precisely the same sacrifice of income. Therefore the division of the diocese was again urged upon the Government and at last relief was granted but not in the manner as was requested. The endeavours of the Bishop to obtain this object resulted in the consecration of the Archdeacon Mountain, who was at that time in England in connection therewith, under the title of Bishop of Montreal.

The ceremony was performed by the Archbishop of Canterbury, at the Chapel of Lambeth Palace, on the 14th Feb., 1836.

The diocese was not divided, nor was any See erected at Montreal, but the new Bishop, with no separate jurisdiction, nor salary, was simply appointed to assist Bishop Stewart, by a commission from him, to such an extent as might be necessary, thus relieving him of the charge of the Lower Province and also assisting in the Upper. Bishop Mountain had also power to administer the affairs of the diocese in the event of his surviving the former till a successor to the See of Quebec should be appointed.

Bishop Mountain remained in England till the end of July and arrived in Quebec on Sunday, 11th September.

On the following Sunday the letters patent of the Bishop of Montreal and also his commission from the Bishop of Quebec appointing him Coadjutor, were read in the Cathedral after the Nicene Creed.

The health of Bishop Stewart had become so enfeebled

that he went to England that fall and died in London at
the residence of his nephew, the Earl of Galloway, and was
buried in the family vault, at the cemetery on the Harrow
Road. The *Quebec Gazette* thus relates :—"In every office
" that he filled, from that of missionary in the woods to that
" which placed him at the head of the Church in Canada,
" he was alike humble, charitable, laborious, devoted, full of
" ardent zeal for the glory of his heavenly Master and over-
" flowing with benevolence to men. He was a shining ex-
" ample of the efficiency of the faith of the Gospel, and in
" the approaches of dissolution, it was that faith, and not
" any reliance upon himself or his own performances, which
" sustained and refreshed him. During his episcopate the
" Church in Canada had continued to progress ; when he
" left the diocese the Clergy numbered eighty-five, of whom
" thirty-four were in the Lower Province."

The Bishop of Montreal, under that title, now presided
over the diocese of Quebec. In May, 1838, Bishop Mountain removed from town to Marchmont, on the St. Louis
Road, Quebec, where he resided for about four years.

The laying of the corner stone of the Rectory or Parsonage
House took place on 12th July, 1841, and is thus recorded
in the columns of the *Quebec Mercury* :—

" On the 12th instant, at 5 o'clock, P.M., was laid the
" corner stone of a Rectory House in the Parsonage lot ad-
" joining the church yard of the Cathedral of this city, by the
" Right Reverend the Lord Bishop of Montreal, in presence
" of the Church-Wardens, the vestry and some members of
" the Congregation. In a cavity of the stone prepared for
" that purpose, and lined and covered with glass, were
" deposited some gold, silver and copper coins of Queen
" Victoria, William IV, and George IV, with two copies of
" the latest Quebec newspapers and a parchment with the
" following inscription, which was read aloud by the Lord
" Bishop, previous to its being deposited :

" This stone was laid
on the 12th day of July, 1841.

The lot having been previously granted by the Crowll.
and the erection of a Parsonage house having been
undertaken by the Select Vestry :

G. J. Mountain, D.D., Lord Bishop of Montreal,
being the Rector,

The Reverend George Mackie, A.B., curate,

T. Trigge and R. Symes, Esquires,

Church Wardens ;

and

The Hon. Geo. Pemberton.	The Hon. W. Walker,
J. Leaycraft,	N. Freer,
J. Bonner,	R. Wainwright,
W. Phillips,	J. Racey,
W. McTavish,	J. B. Forsyth,
H. Jessop, Esquires.	H. Gowan, Esquires.

The Select Vestry.

T. Hacker and E. Taylor Fletcher, architects.

Messrs. Fielders and Smith, builders.

" Except the Lord built the house their labour is but lost that build it.

" May He enable those who are to inhabit here, to build up their
" followers upon the Chief Corner Stone of Zion .as a spiritual house, to
" offer up spiritual sacrifices, acceptable to God by Jesus Christ."

It is in contemplation to add a wing to the above mentioned building, to be fitted up as a chapel for occasional
minor services and meetings of the Congregation for religious purposes, as soon as the voluntary contributions of the
members of the Church shall warrant its commencement.
The Rectory was completed in 1842, and the Bishop, by an
arrangement with the vestry, voluntarily agreed to pay an
annual rent of £100 and resided there. This money was
devoted to the payment of the balance of the cost of the
building, which in a few years was paid off, and the annual
rent allowed to accumulate, when a resolution was passed
at a meeting of the Vestry, held on 31st October, 1855,
creating it the Rectory Endowment Fund.

During his visitation to the city of Montreal in 1842, the
Bishop organized the Church Society of the Diocese of

Quebec, at a large meeting convened there on the 7th July for that purpose.

St. Peter's Chapel having been condemned as unsafe, the property was returned to the former proprietor, when the present site on St. Valier street was purchased, and the corner stone laid on 25th July, 1842.

On his return from Red River, the Bishop laid the foundation stone of Bishop's College, Lennoxville, 18th September, 1844, and on 1st November, he consecrated the Chapel adjoining the Rectory, naming it All Saints' Chapel.

The paid choir seems to have been abolished for it is stated in the Vestry minutes : that in 1844, Lieut. Whitman, of H. M. 1st Royals, furnished a choir from the regiment, and that on their leaving Quebec, a testimonial was presented to him and his choir for their valuable services; also, that Mr. Archibald Campbell then organized the voluntary choir and received the thanks of the Easter meeting of the Congregation, on the 24th March, 1845.

That year, two disastrous conflagrations ravaged the city, the first on the 28th May, swept St. Rochs, when St. Peter's Chapel was burnt; and on the 28th June, St. John's suburbs was consumed, St. Mathew's Chapel sharing the same fate as St. Peter's ; but help came from afar, for the Society for Promoting Christian Knowledge, generously granted £100 sterling to each of those chapels, as soon as funds would be raised for re-building them, also a grant of prayer books to the value of £20 towards replacing those lost in the fires.

St. Peter's was re-opened on 20th September, 1846, but the corner stone of St. Matthew's was not laid till 25th July, 1848.

A new organ was imported from England for the Cathedral at a cost of £872, and was opened on Sunday, 19th September, 1847. The old instrument was sold to the Roman Catholic Church at Lotbinière, when it was repaired and proved to be an excellent instrument. It is still in use, (1891.)

During the summer of 1847, thousands of emigrants arrived at Grosse-Isle, the quarantine station, with a virulent epidemic of ship or typhus fever raging amongst them. It was so fatal that some 5000 of them lie buried on the island. The Bishop took his turn along with the clergy of the Diocese in ministering to these afflicted people, and six devoted servants of God fell victims to the disease, the Reverend Messrs. Dawes, Chaderton, Lloyd, Willoughby, Morris and Anderson.

A portion of the burying ground on Charlesbourg road, attached to the Marine Hospital for the burial of strangers, was set apart for the Church of England, and was consecrated by the Bishop on 9th November, 1848.

The long sought for division of the diocese was accomplished, and on 25th July, 1850, Dr. Fulford was consecrated in Westminster Abbey, Bishop of Montreal. *

Fresh letters patent had been issued appointing Bishop Mountain to the See of Quebec, and he was formally enthroned in the Cathedral on 21st September.

The Diocese of Quebec comprises the county of St. Maurice and all east thereof on the North Shore of the St. Lawrence to the Atlantic ; on the South Shore the counties of Nicolet, Drummond, Richmond, Sherbrooke, Stanstead and all east including Gaspesia and the Magdalen Islands.

St. Michael's Chapel, opposite Mount Hermon Cemetery, was built in 1854.

In 1857, the Cathedral underwent a thorough repair and was freshly painted. The pews, which were uncomfortably high, were lowered to 3 feet 3 inches and book boards placed in each. All Saints' Chapel was repaired at the same time and six stalls for the Bishop and clergy put in and the walls were wainscotted. Towards the close of 1858, the Revd.

---

* The last Canadian Bishop consecrated in England, was the Right Reverend Ashton Oxenden, Lord Bishop of Montreal, and Metropolitan of Canada, who was consecrated at Westminster Abbey, on Sunday, 8th August, 1869, by the Archbishop of Canterbury, assisted by the Bishops of London, Rochester and Ely.

" Official " Dr. George Mackie returned to England, and the Bishop appointed the Revd. S. S. Wood, to be his examining chaplain, and the Revd. George Vernon Houseman, assistant minister at the Cathedral.

It will be interesting, as a memento, to record the names of the several clergymen who preached at different times in the Cathedral, from the year 1840 to 1858 :—the Reverend Messrs. W. Chaderton, C. L. F. Haensel, F. G. Lundy, R. R. Burrage, G. Mackie, H. D. Sewell, E. W. Sewell, F. J. Torrance, Jos. Brown, G. Cowell, W. B. Robinson, W. W. Wait, C. Bancroft, E. Senkler, E. C. Parkin, J. Simpson, J. Cornwall, R. G. Plees, G. Percy, A. W. Mountain, C. Stewart, J. Pennyfather, W. Wicks, J. Adamson, R. Carden, H. Roe, W. King, T. Carry, S. Jones, A. J. Woolryche, Dr. Hellmuth, Charles Hamilton and J. Mombert.

The petition to the Imperial Government to legalize the holding of Diocesan and Provincial Synods was granted and the sanction of the Local Legislatures to the action of these Synods was also obtained, hence the first Synod of the Diocese of Quebec was held on the 6th July, 1859.

At the instance of the Lord Bishop, the Government of Canada provided and fitted up a Chapel in the east wing of the Marine Hospital for the use of the sick members of the Church of England being patients there. The chaplaincy had been established on the 20th February, 1854, and maintained by a grant of $200 per annum from the " Society for the Propagation of the Gospel in Foreign Parts," and a salary of $144 from the Government which appointed the Chaplain at the nomination of the Bishop of Quebec. The chapel was ready for service in 1859, and on 23rd November, the Chaplain, Revd. Gilbert Percy, petitioned the Bishop to consecrate it, which ceremony was performed on 7th December, 1859, and named St. Luke's Chapel. The hospital was closed in the fall of 1889, by the Department of Marine, and in the spring of 1891, was under certain conditions transferred to the city for a civic hospital.

His Royal Highness Albert Edward Prince of Wales
visited Canada in the summer of 1860, and as a memento of
his attending divine service at the Cathedral on Sunday,
19th August, presented to the Bishop a handsome Bible for
the use of that church, and also a donation of £200 for
Bishop's College, Lennoxville, thus founding the Prince of
Wales' scholarship.

On the 2nd August, 1862, Bishop Mountain completed
the 50th anniversary of his ministry, when an address was
presented to him by the Diocesan Synod, in the Lecture
Hall, now Tara Hall, St. Anne street, and at half-past ten
divine service was celebrated in the Cathedral. A very
large congregation was present, including Lord Monck,
Governor-General, and thirty-five of the Diocesan Clergy, an
eloquent sermon was preached by the Right Revd. Dr. John
Williams, Assistant Bishop of Connecticut. At the close of
the service, the Bishop attended by the Clergy and Congregation, proceeded to the Finlay Asylum, on St. Foy Road,
which had only been recently finished, and formally opened
that institution with a special service.

Towards the end of December, Bishop Mountain took ill
and died at his residence, Woodfield, on 6th January, 1863,
at the age of 73 years, and the funeral took place at 10.30
A.M., of Tuesday, 13th. There were many who regretted
that the Bishop was not buried in the Cathedral, beside his
father, but it was according to his own expressed wish that
he rests at the side of his wife in Mount Hermon.

The churchmen of Quebec placed to his memory, in the
chancel of the Cathedral, that beautiful stained glass window representing the Ascension, Transfiguration and Baptism of our Lord, and inscribed thereon. " To the glory of
" God, and in grateful remembrance of George Jehoshaphat
" Mountain, D.D., sometime Bishop of this diocese, whom
" the grace of Christ, enabled to fulfil the duties of a long

" ministry to the advancement of his church and the
" lasting benefit of many souls." O.B., MDCCCLXIII,
Aet. LXXIII.

Hitherto the appointment of Canadian Bishops rested
with the British Government, but on the 13th June, 1856,
an act was passed by both Houses of the Provincial Parlia-
ment, (19 and 20 Victoria, cap. 141), to enable the members
of the united Church of England and Ireland in Canada to
meet in Synod, and the Synods of the several dioceses
were permitted to elect their own Bishops, Her Majesty the
Queen ratifying the appointment. Therefore by article 9
of the constitution of the Synod of the diocese of Quebec,
the assistant-minister of the Cathedral called a special meeting of the Synod for the 4th March, 1863, for the purpose of
electing a successor to the late Bishop.

At the eleventh ballot, forty-one clergymen and sixty-two
of the lay delegates being present, the Revd. J. W. Williams,
M.A., professor of Belles-Lettres in the University of Bishop's
College, Lennoxville, and Rector of the Junior Department,
was declared by the secretaries, Bishop elect, by a clerical
vote of 28 and a lay vote of 52. It was moved by Revd.
H. Roe and seconded by Mr. H. S. Scott, that the election
be unanimously concurred in, which was carried by all
standing. It was then moved by Mr. George Irvine,
seconded by Revd. Charles Hamilton and carried :— " That
" the form of petition recommended by the Provincial
" Synod be adopted, and after having been signed by the
" President, (Revd. G. V. Housman) and Secretaries, (Revd.
" C. Hamilton, Clerical, and J. B. Forsyth, Esq., Lay Secret-
" ary), on behalf of the Synod, be transmitted through the
" proper channels to Her Majesty the Queen."

Her Majesty's mandate arrived on the 16th June, 1863,
and the consecration was arranged to take place on Sunday,
the 21st inst., thus giving time for the Metropolitan, and all

the Bishops in Canada, as well as the clergy and lay delegates of the Synod to be present. *

The Revd. G. V. Houseman, curate of the Cathedral, was appointed ‡ Rector of Quebec.

Among other objects of interest in the Cathedral, are those old tattered colours, bearing the records of the battles in which H. M. 69th Regt. was present. On the return of the 69th from repelling the Fenian invasion in June, 1870, on the Huntingdon Frontier, H. R. H. Prince Arthur, then Lieutenant in the P. C. O. Rifle Brigade, presented the Regiment with a new stand of colours. The old ones were, on the 22nd, deposited in the Cathedral with an interesting and imposing ceremony :—The Rector and clergy had taken their position within the altar rails, when the Captain commanding the escort knocked at the main door ; the Rector then desired the Church Wardens, R. H. Wurtele and George Hall, Esquires, to ascertain who knocked, and on being so informed,—Captain Charlton was admitted, and on reaching the chancel thus addressed the Rector :—

" I have been commanded by Lt.-Col. George Bagot, to " repair with the old colours of the 69th Regiment, under a " sufficient escort to this Cathedral, in the hope that its

* The Revd. James William Williams is the son of the Revd. D. Williams, rector of Banghurst, Hants. He is cousin to the Revd. Isaac Williams, rector of Hincheombe, the well known commentator and sacred poet, and also a connection of Sir George Prevost. He was born in 1825, at Overton, Hants, and was educated under Dr. Perry, at the grammar school of Crewkerne in Somersetshire. At the age of nineteen, he was sent out to New Zealand, to assist in the government survey of that colony. After a residence there of not quite two years, he returned to England and resumed his studies for the university. He matriculated at Pembroke College, Oxford, taking the degree of B.A., in 1851, and soon afterwards that of M.A. He was ordained by the Bishop of Oxford and presented by him to the curacy of Highwycombe, Bucks. Subsequently he was appointed one of the classical masters of the well known College of Leamington, and for about a year before leaving England, was curate of Huish Champflower, in Somersetshire, when he was appointed Rector of Bishop's College School, Lennoxville, and entered upon his duties in August, 1857, to which was added the professorship of Belles-Lettres in the University.

‡ Canon XIII of the Synod of the Diocese of Quebec.

" authorities will permit these venerable emblems of loyalty,
" Christianity and civilization to find a fitting resting place
" within the walls of this sacred building, in the midst of
" a loyal and God-fearing population." To which the
Rector replied:—

" In form Lt.-Col. Bagot, that we receive these colours as a
" sacred trust, not only as emblems of loyalty, Christianity
" and civilization, but in remembrance of a Regiment which
" has been conspicuous in repelling a recent invasion of this
" Province. Whose conduct has been characterized by a
" singular regard of order and regularity, and which by its
" general bearing, has deservedly won the highest esteem
" of every member of this community."

The clergy then in procession advanced to the main door
of the Cathedral and returned followed by the escort and
colours, the familiar strain of " Home, Sweet Home," pealing
from the organ. When the clergy had resumed their places
within the railing, the colours were handed to the Rector,
the escort presented arms, and the National Anthem was
played on the organ. The service then opened with a
hymn, followed by appropriate prayers and concluded with
an eloquent address by the Rector.

The organ, which had been in use since 1847, was found
to be very much out of order and that it would be advisable
to obtain a modern instrument: for that purpose, an influ-
ential member * of the Congregation generously placed five
thousand dollars in the hands of the Church Wardens. The
services of Mr. Warren, organ builder, were called in and
it was found that many of the old pipes were in perfect
condition ; these were utilised and, with the new ones, were
enclosed in a handsome new case, thus making a fine instrument valued at $7,000. It was opened in 1871, and pro-
nounced by experts to be one unexcelled in sweetness and
volume of tone.

---

* R. R. Dobell, Esq.

By virtue of the "Act respecting Rectories," the appointment of the Rector of Quebec was vested in the Church Society of the Diocese of Quebec, which right it exercised on 14th January, 1863. Subsequently the Synod of the Diocese passed a Canon, giving to the Congregation of the Cathedral the right of electing thirteen of their number to form a Board of Concurrence for the appointment of a Rector of Quebec, and to obtain this right, three-fourths of the Vestry present at any Easter meeting must unite in requesting the Bishop to permit the Congregation to place themselves under the Canon.

At the Easter meeting of 6th April, 1885, a committee was named to take the necessary steps to have such appointments come under this Canon, whose report was unanimously adopted at the Easter meeting of 26th April, 1886, and the necessary resolution was passed at the annual meeting of the Church Society, 2nd February, 1887, and ratified by the Bishop.

The Jubilee of Her Imperial Majesty, Queen Victoria, was celebrated on the 21st June, 1887, in the parish of Quebec by a united service in the Cathedral. A very large congregation filled the church, all the clergy of the parish being present; those taking part in the service were the Revds. H. J. Petry, Richardson, Rexford, Von Iffland and Bareham. The Revd. M. M. Fothergill preached an eloquent sermon from Proverbs XXIX. 2, after which the jubilee version of the National Anthem was sung amid the chiming of the Cathedral bells and the booming of a Royal salute from the guns of the Citadel.

The Rector of Quebec, Revd. George Vernon Housman died at the Rectory, on 26th September, 1887, at the age of 67 years. He was a graduate of St. John's College, Cambridge, and was appointed assistant minister at the Cathedral in October, 1858, and at the death of Bishop Mountain, was inducted Rector of Quebec.

According to section 8 of the XIII Canon of the Synod, the Board of Concurrence for appointing a Rector was elected by the Congregation * on the 15th October, which resulted in the unanimous nomination of the Revd. R. W. Norman, D.D., Canon of Montreal, who accepted the office, and was inducted Rector of Quebec, in the Cathedral, by the Bishop, on Sunday, 18th March, 1888.

† Dr. Norman was educated at King's College School, London, England, and received his degree of M.A., at Oxford. He became assistant and afterwards head master of Radley College, which position he held from 1852 to 1866, when he came to Canada on a visit, but finding the climate so beneficial to his constitution decided to remain, and for a time assisted the Revd. Mr. Wood, of St. John's Church, at Montreal, as a volunteer. Subsequently he was appointed assistant minister at the Church of St. James, where he remained for many years. Leaving this he accepted a call to that of St. Mathias, Cote St. Antoine, from which he came to Christ Church Cathedral. Outside of the Ministry Dr. Norman's chief work has been the promotion of higher education ; he became a member of the Protestant School Board of Montreal and, since 1881, held the position of chairman ; he is an honorary and also Governor's Fellow of McGill University, Vice-Chancellor of Bishop's College, Lennoxville, a member of the Protestant Council of Public Instruction for this Province, and classical examiner in the Medical Faculty of Bishop's College ; was appointed Canon in 1878, and received the degree of D.C.L. from Bishop's College. Dr. Norman has been Hon. Clerical Secretary of the Provincial Synod since 1880, and is also Commissary of the Diocese of Algoma.

---

* Board of Concurrence consisted of Messrs. W. Rae, R. H. Smith, J. Dunbar, Q. C., R. R. Dobell, T. Beckett, E. J. Hale, Edwin A. Jones, J. Stevenson, R. Turner, H. M. Price, W. C. Scott, C. P. Champion and Sir W. C. Meredith.

† From " *Montreal Star.*"

The establishment of a Capitular Body to the Cathedral had been provided for at the fifth session of the Diocesan Synod, but the several appointments had not been made, when at the 25th anniversary of his consecration on 21st June, 1888, the Bishop notified in his charge to the Synod, then in session, that the Dean and Chapter would be appointed, also that he had nominated the Rector of Quebec, the Revd. R. W. Norman, D.D., D.C.L., Dean, and the Revd. Henry Roe, M.A., D.D , Archdeacon of the Diocese. Before the adjournment, he gave the following notification to the Synod :—

" I now inform the Synod, that the agreement between " the Bishop and the Rector and Church-Wardens of the " Parish of Quebec, indicated in the Canon concerning the ' Capitular Body, has been signed and sealed ; and that I " have appointed the Revd. Dr. Norman, to be Dean, and " the Revd. John Foster, M.A., the Revd. Thomas Richard-" son, the Revd. George Thorneloe, M.A., and the Revd. A. A. " Von Iffland, M.A., to be Canons of the Cathedral of " Quebec. Mr. Richardson and Mr. Von lfland to be " Resident Canons, Mr. Foster and Mr. Thorneloe to be " Rural Canons."

On his Lordship's return from England, the Dean and Chapter were installed in the Cathedral on the 21st September, with the usual ceremony.

Before closing this monograph, it will be interesting to record and describe the various monuments placed on the walls of the sacred edifice, to the memory of Quebec's prominent citizens and public men who worshipped in this Cathedral Church.

On the floor behind the pulpit is a brass plate whereon is written :—

" Beneath are deposited the mortal
remains of Charles Duke of Richmond
Lenox and Aubigny
The Monument to his memory is placed
In the North gallery of this Church."

This tablet to the memory of the tenth English Governor General of Canada, is situated between the first and second windows, and is one of the finest in the Church, the design being a weeping female figure between crossed standards, surmounted by a sword and wreath, with this inscription beneath.*

Sacred to the memory of Charles
Fourth Duke of Richmond, Lenox and Aubigny ;
Knight of the Most Honorable Order of the Garter,
Lord Lieutenant and Vice-Admiral of the County of Sussex ;
High Steward of the City of Chichester ;
A General in the Army, and Colonel of the 35th Regiment
and of the Royal Sussex Militia.
Governor General and Commander in Chief of Canada,
and over all His Majesty's possessions in North America,
Who died at Richmond in Upper Canada
on the 29th of August, 1819, in the 55th year of his age.

Inside the chancel rails are three monuments of white marble on black ground. The principal one being that to the Right Revd. Jacob Mountain, D. D., first Bishop of Quebec. The bust is in the Episcopal dress, the head inclining forward and from the shoulders up is in alto relievo, resting on a pedestal on which are engraved the arms of the Diocese, and beneath, this latin inscription :

Hic jacet
Vir admodum reverendus
Jacob Mountain, S.T.P.
Episcopus Quebecensis,
Ecclesiae Anglicanae,
in Canadis fundator,
Qui obiit A.S., MDCCCXXV,
Ætatis suae, LXXV,
Episcopatus, XXXIII ;
Præsul in divino munere obeundo,
Promptus, fidelis, indefessus ;
in Memoriam
Viri egregii,
et sibi Carissimi
hoc marmor
Conjux et liberi
Superstites
P. C.

* Copy of the Burial Register is in Appendix B.

Beside it is a full length figure of religion clasping a Bible to her breast, and above, the emblematical designs of the Cross and Crozier.

Next to this is one of recent date : —

In grateful and affectionate remembrance of the
Revd. George Vernon Housman, M. A.
Born at St. Peters, Guernsey, October 15th, 1820.
Died September 26th, 1887,
In the forty-third year of his ministry.
He was for over
a quarter of a century the faithful priest
of this Church and Rector of Quebec.
This tablet was erected at the request of his parishioners.
" Behold my witness is in heaven and he that voucheth for me is
on high." Job. XVI-19.

On the opposite wall is that to the second Bishop of Quebec :—

In memory of the
Honorable and Right Revd. Charles James Stewart, D.D.,
Bishop of Quebec,
Third son of John, seventh Earl of Galloway,
Sometime fellow of all Soul's College, Oxford,
And Rector of Overton Longville, Huntingdonshire, England.
In the year MDCCCVII, he devoted himself
To the office of a Missionary in Canada,
Which he filled in succession at Philipsburg,
Frelighsburg and Charleston
In the Eastern Townships.
In MDCCCXIX, he was appointed,
Visiting Missionary of the Diocese of Quebec,
And on the vacancy of that See,
Was consecrated thereto, at Lambeth Chapel, January 1st, MDCCCXXVI.
Animated as he was by a fervent and unabated zeal.
In the discharge of the duties of his high and holy calling,
His ministrations of the Blessed Gospel was distinguished,
By humility of mind, by universal charity.
And by an unreserved dedication of all his powers,
In reliance for sufficiency upon the Divine Grace,
To the Glory of God, and the best interest of man.
In the faith and hope of them that die in the Lord.
He departed this life, July XIIIth, MDCCCXXXVII.
In the LXIIIrd year of his age,
And is buried in the family vault of the Earl of Galloway,
In the cemetery, Harrow Road, near London.
In testimony of affectionate veneration for his many virtues
And in gratitude to God,
For the benefits thereby conferred upon this Diocese,
This tablet was erected by public subscription, MDCCCXLI.

On the south wall near the Vestry door is a plain marble slab, in memory of one of Quebec's old Citizens.

Sacred to the memory of
Hammond Gowen,
who was born at the village of Medford, near Boston,
On the 6th July, 1784
And departed this life at Quebec,
On the 18th April, 1864.
His end was peace, looking for the mercy of
Our Lord Jesus Christ unto eternal life.

———

Next to this is a double monument surmounted by the crest of the Prince Consort's Own Rifle Brigade, having at the base two bugles joined by wreath :-

Sacred
to the memory of
Arthur Wilson Patten, Lieutenant
The Prince Consort's Own Rifle Brigade,
Died in Quebec, 2nd January, 1866,
aged 24 years
and
Robert Dundas, Ensign,
The Prince Consort's Own Rifle Brigade.
Died in Quebec, 19th September, 1865.
Aged 21 years,
Erected by their
Brother Officers.

———

Alongside of this are mementos of two brave men who lost their lives while on duty striving to stay the ravages of fires devasting portions of this city.

A white marble cross bears the inscription :—

Sacred to the memory of
Lieut. H. E. Baines, Royal Artillery,
Who died on 27th October, 1866, aged 26 years,
From injuries received when on duty at the great
fire in Quebec, on the 14th October, 1866.
Erected by his brother officers.

———

Beside it is a finely finished brass plate. The sides are fringed with a border of maple leaves, and at the very bottom stands the word " Canada." At the top is the Motto : " Quo fas et gloria ducunt." Immediately below this is the Royal Crown over a Field Artillery Gun, underneath which is inscribed :—

" In memory of
Major CHARLES JOHN SHORT,
Commanding " B " Battery
Regiment of Canadian Artillery,
who lost his life in the discharge of his duty
at the
Great fire at St. Sauveur, Quebec, 16th May,
1889,
Aged 42 years.
This tablet is erected by his brother-officers of the Regiment,
in affectionate remembrance of a brave and gallant comrade. "

On the north side between the first and second windows are two tablets, as follows :—

In memory of Charlotte Saxton,
The beloved wife of Dr. George Mellis Douglas
who departed this life,
the 24th May, 1852,
aged 32 years.
Therefore my heart is glad, and my
glory rejoiceth ; my flesh also shall rest
in Hope. Psalm XVI. Ver. 9.

Sacred
to the memory of
Maria, Cornelia Westrene,
wife of
James A. Sewell, M.D.
A fond wife, a tender mother, a sincere friend,
She lived loving and beloved : and
Died in the full hope of a Resurrection
to Eternal life.
After a short attack of Asiatic cholera,
On the 18th day of July, 1849,
aged 38 years.
Unto the Lord belong the issues of death. Psalm 68-20.

Between the second and third windows are two slabs on which are the following inscriptions :—

In memory of
John Robert N. Symes, Esq.,
Born at Camberwell,
Surrey, England, 6th January, 1794,
Arrived at Quebec in May, 1816,
Where he resided many years and
died at
Meaford, Canada West,
10th December, 1858.
He was magistrate at Grosse-Isle,
In 1847, during the ship fever,
And on several occasions
Church Warden of this Parish.
His constant aim was to do good.
This tablet is erected
By the St. George's Society of Quebec,
Of which he was Treasurer for sixteen years,
That his memory may not be forgotten.

Sacred to the memory of
John Christie,
Sergeant-Major 54th Regiment (son of Sergeant Christie,
late of the same corps). Born at Birr in Scotland.
Died at Quebec, 7th January, 1853, aged 33 years.

This tablet is erected by the Officers, Non-Commissioned officers and privates of the 54th Regiment, to record the sense of their loss and in testimony of their esteem for him as a good Soldier, and a sincere Christian.

Between the third and fourth windows is the following on a marble slab :

In memory of
Maria Margaret
wife of George T. Woodman, M. D.,
and daughter of the late William Stevenson of Quebec,
Died at sea on the passage to England, 15th November, 1864.
" Ho every one that thirsteth come ye to the waters, and
He that hath no money, come ye buy and eat, yea come buy wine,
and milk without money and without price."—Isaiah LV-1.

Two brass plates are thus engraved :—

In memory of
Honorable George Pemberton, M.L.C.
Born at Dublin, August 2nd, 1795.
Died at Quebec, February 21st, 1869

In memory of George Tudor Pemberton,
Born April 27th, 1838.   Died May 10th, 1882

Let us mount the stairs and see what memorials the
north gallery contains ; to the right side of the eastern door
are two tablets, the upper one is :

Sacred to the memory
of
Captain Thomas Impett,
late of the 32nd Regiment,
who died at Quebec,
on the 15th February, 1833,
Aged 40 years, 5 months.
This monument was erected by his
Brother officers as a token
of their esteem and regard.

Underneath is one surmounted by reclining standards
over them a mural crown.

Sacred to the memory
of Lieutenant General Peter Hunter,
Lieutenant Governor of Upper Canada and Commander in chief
of His Majesty's Forces in both the Canadas ;
who died at Quebec on the XXI of August, MDCCCV,
aged LIX years.
His life was spent in the service of his King and country,
of the various stations, both civil and military which he filled
He discharged the duties with spotless integrity,
unwearied zeal and successful abilities.
This memorial to a brother whose
mortal part rests in the adjacent place of burial,
is erected by John Hunter, M.D., of London.

Over the door is one,

Sacred
to the memory of the children of
John and Elizabeth Davidson.
John Hamilton,
who died at Chambly,
on the 8th February, 1830, aged 12.
Henry Edward,
who died at Quebec,
on the 24th May, 1838, aged 26.
Frances Isabella,
The beloved wife of Stephen Walcott,
who died at Torquay, in England ;
on the 20th February, 1849, aged 35.
" They all fell asleep looking unto Jesus.
The Lord gave and the Lord hath taken
away : Blessed be the name of the Lord."
Watch ye therefore, for ye know not,
When the Master of the House cometh.

To the left of the door is a double memorial tablet, the
right half of it contains the following :—

In memory of
Lt.-Col. George Augustus Eliot,
late of the 68th Regiment,
Major of Brigade to H. M. Forces in Canada,
who died at Quebec on the 6th August, 1835,
aged 51 years.
His affectionate widow
records in this tablet her own irreparable loss :
The name of her husband,
she trusts has been registered in heaven,
with that of his only child,
by whose side his own remains are deposited,
in the burying ground,
adjoining to St. Matthew's chapel,
within the vault of the family of Freer.
Alike in war and peace.
He served, most devotedly, his earthly King :
But he was not called away till his heart
Had been given to his heavenly Lord,
And he died in full and blessed reliance
Upon the Saviour of sinners.

The left half of this slab relates as follows :

In memory of
Augustus Lionel Eliot
only child of
Lieut.-Colonel G. A. Eliot,
and of Jane his wife.
Who departed this life on
the 30th June, 1834,
in the 18th year of his age.
Cut off by a lingering disease
in the first flower of his youth,
with all the pleasures of this life
just opening to his view.
He bore his suffering with meekness,
Grieved not for himself but for his parents,
and resigned his spirit freely
to Him who giveth and taketh away,
leaving an example,
of the efficacy of faith in Christ,
Through whom alone
He looked for Salvation.
His last prayer was
Lord Jesus come quickly.

The first window in this gallery is of stained glass, the subject being " The Good Shepherd," with the inscription :

George Burns Symes, born January 20th, 1803, died June 12th, 1863.

This window is erected to his memory by his only child, Clara, Marquise de Bassano.

The space between the second and third window is filled with a mural tablet on which is engraved the following, underneath the Stewart arms and motto "Nobilis Ira."

Sacred
to
the memory of the Honorable
John Stewart,
a member of Her Majesty's
Executive and Legislative Councils,
of this Province,
Commissioner
of the Jesuits' Estates
and master of the " Trinity House."
Born at
Musselburgh, Scotland, 24th November, 1773.
Died at Beauvoir,
near this city, 5th June, 1858.
During a residence in Quebec of sixty-four years,
He discharged various offices of public trust,
with singular prudence, and unsullied integrity,
as his life was marked by uprightness.
So his end was peace,
Looking for the mercy of Our Lord Jesus Christ unto eternal life.
Also
In memory of his beloved wife,
Eliza Maria
Daughter of Colonel James Green, formerly of the 26th Cameronians,
She died at Bandon Lodge, near Quebec,
8th March, 1828, aged 36 years.
The memory of the just is blessed.

Between the third and fourth windows is a fine large monument surmounted by an urn with a drapery partially covering it.

Sacred
to the memory of
James Hunt,
born at Dartmouth, England,
on the 9th of September, 1779.
Died at Quebec,
after a residence of 44 years,
on the 31st of March, 1847,
and to his wife,
Mary S. Garland,
Born at Molescombe, Devon, England,
on the 20th of July, 1784.
Died at Quebec,
on 28th of December, 1866.

————

Between the fourth and fifth windows are two tablets, the lower one a memento of one of the founders of the Literary and Historical Society of Quebec :—

Sacred
to the memory of
John Charlton Fisher, LL.D.,
26 years Queen's Printer for Lower Canada,
who died at sea.
On board the steamship " Sarah Sands."
in returning from England,
on the 10th day of August, 1849,
aged 55 years,
and of
Elinor Isabella Auchmuty,
his wife,
who departed this life
on the 22nd day of January, 1860,
aged 63 years.

————

Just over the above is one,

Sacred to the memory of
J. E. Haig,
aged 18 years,
Midshipman of H. M. S. "Vindictive,
who fell overboard and was drowned,
while the ship was at anchor off this city,
on the night of the 24th September, 1846.
This tablet was erected by the officers
of the ship as a token of the great esteem
in which he was universally held.

———

Passing over to the south gallery we find the following
mural tablets and memorial windows. To the left of the
door leading to the vestry is one on a ground of grey marble,
inscribed as follows :

" Blessed are the Dead,
which die in the Lord."
Sacred to the memory of
The Honorable Carleton Thomas Monckton,
fifth son of Robert Arundel, fourth Viscount Galway.
By his wife Elizabeth, daughter of Daniel Matthew, Esq., of Felix Hall,
Essex, and great nephew of the Honorable Brigadier General Monckton,
who succeeded to the command of the British Army,
upon the death of General Wolfe at the splendid victory
achieved on the heights of Abraham, 13th September, A.D., 1759.
At the age of fifteen, he entered the army and served in Spain,
And at the battle of Waterloo was a Lieutenant.
He for some years afterwards became a Captain
in the 24th Regiment of Infantry which he accompanied to Canada,
and died after a short illness at Quebec on the 10th May, 1830,
in the 34th year of his age, beloved by his brother officers,
and sincerely lamented by all who knew him.
This tablet was erected by his sorrowing brother and sisters,
as a testimony of their fond affection to one
most justly dear to them.
And in the humble hope that through faith in Christ Jesus,
The only Saviour, they together with him.
may be blessed as are those that die in the Lord.

———

Over the Vestry door is one whose inscription reads thus :

Sacred to the memory of
Robert Dunn, Esq.,
Third son of
The late Honorable Thomas Dunn,
who departed this life January 13th, 1825,
in the 37th year of his age,
and also to his two daughters,
Mary Henrietta Margaret Dunn.
Born 28th October, 1823.   Died 25th May, 1832.
and
Frances Sarah Dunn.
Born 31st May, 1825.   Died 22nd November, 1845.
In the midst of life we are in Death.

———

To the right of the door stands one,

Sacred to the memory of
Houston Thomson Cochran
wife of Andrew William Cochran of Quebec, Esquire.
Born the 29th day of June, 1795, died the 15th day of June, 1837.
Blameless in her every relation of life.
Patient, pious and resigned under manifold afflictions.
She held the noiseless tenor of her way in Christian faith and life
and peace.
Her husband has placed this tablet in good remembrance of those virtues,
which during nineteen years, formed the blessing of his life ;
and in the cherished hope of being reunited to her in that eternal rest,
where sorrow and separation shall be no more.
" Her virtues walked their tranquil round,
Nor made a pause, nor left a void :
and her eternal Master found
the given talents well employed."

———

Next comes a beautiful stained glass window containing a representation of the Good Samaritan. Above this group is an angel holding the inscription "Blessed are the merciful." Below it, another angel with the words "Go and do thou likewise."

In memory of Archibald Campbell, H. M. Notary.
Born 29th June, 1790, died 16th July, 1862.

———

The next window is also of stained glass representing the "Children coming to Jesus." This group is surmounted by two angels bearing a Crown and the inscription. "Her children rise up and call her blessed."

To the glory of God and in loving memory of Agnes Campbell.
Born 1793, died December 23rd, 1880.

M. D. N.   W. D. C.

———

Between these two windows is a monument of exquisite workmanship, having a figure of a dying man, supported by a woman with extended arm pointing upwards. In the man's left hand is a book on which is written " And now Lord what wait I for ? My hope is in thee." Psalm 39, ver. 7. Underneath this group is inscribed :—

In memory of Thomas Dunn, Esq., of Durham, in England,
who departed this life on the 15th April, A.D , 1818,
in the 88th year of his age.
During his long residence in this country,
where he established himself soon after the conquest.
He held several important situations under government.
He was one of the original members of the Legislative and
Executive Councils.
In which last capacity, during two different vacant intervals
He administered the Government of this Province.
His known integrity and goodness,
procured him the confidence and respect of the community ;
And he was eminently possessed of those private qualities
which cause men to be beloved during life,
and lamented in death.

———

Between the next two windows is the following tablet :—

Sacred to the memory of
Mary Anne Jessop,
wife of Henry Jessop, Esq.,
Collector of His Majesty's Customs at this Port.
Who as a wife, daughter and sister,
was a blessing, a solace, and a guide,
and in every other relation of life exemplary.
This tablet was erected by her husband,
In memory of her many virtues,
and in gratitude for past happiness,
which terminated with her life,
After years of unrepining suffering on the 2nd June, 1836.
at the age of 31 years and 7 months.
Oh ! could this fleeting record breathe,
But half the worth bless'd shade beneath,
Then had the monumental stone.
Peer'd with all before it gone.

———

After the third window comes one :—

Sacred
to the memory of
John Racey, M.D.E. and M.R.C.S.E.,
who died on the 25th October, 1847,
of typhus fever contracted in the
conscientious and benevolent discharge
of his professional duties,
aged 38 years and 7 months.
The tribute is erected by his affectionate widow.
Lord remember me when thou comest
into thy kingdom.
Verily I say unto thee ; To-day shalt thou
Be with me in Paradise.

———

The next monument between the fourth and fifth windows is a large one with a helmet and sword cut in relief near the top, whose inscription reads thus :—

Sacred
to the memory of
George S. Montizambert,
Major in H.M. 10th Regiment of Foot,
a native of this city,
who entered the British army,
in 1831.
Served throughout the campaign
of 1843, in Afghanistan,
and was killed
while bravely leading his men
to the assault of an outwork
of the fortress of Mooltan,
in North Western India,
on the 12th September, 1846,
in the 36th year of his age.
" Let us not therefore sorrow even as
others which have no hope.
For we know that Jesus died and rose
again and that even so them also which
sleep in Jesus will God bring with him."

———

Next to the organ, which he loved so well, is a marble slab :—

In memory of
Stephen Codman, Esq.,
a native of Norwich in England,
who was for thirty-six years organist of this church.
He died on the 6th October, 1852,
aged 56 years,
and is buried in the Mount Hermon cemetery, near this city.
This tablet is a tribute from the congregation
to record the sense of their loss.

———

Many eminent ministers of the Church of England have visited Quebec and preached in this Cathedral, among whom were Dean Stanley, 20th October, 1878, the Ven. Archdeacon F. W. Farrar, and Cannon Wilberforce, now Bishop of Newcastle, who during a week in March, 1881, conducted a most successful mission in Quebec, also the Rt.-Revd. C. P. McIlvaine, Bishop of Ohio, and several other dignitaries of the church in the United States.

The several clergymen who, since 1854, have at different times held the position of assistant minister of the Cathedral, were in their order : the Reverends A. W. Mountain, Dr. Percy, G. V. Housman, G. M. Innes, C. F. Thorndyke, C. W. Rawson, Mr. Ridley, Mr. Trotman, and the Revd. H. J. Petry the present incumbent.

At the Easter meeting held in the Church Hall, 30th March, 1891, Edwin A. Jones, Esq., was re-nominated Rector's warden and E. J. Hale, Esq., re-elected warden of the congregation, and the following gentlemen were elected to compose the select vestry for the ensuing year : Messrs. C. P. Champion, R. R. Dobell, R. H. Smith, J. C. More, W. C. Scott, R. Turner, E. H. Wade, H. Staveley, W. M. Macpherson, E. E. Webb, T. Norris and the Hon. H. G. Joly de Lotbinière.

Since 1824, the Cathedral Sunday School had assembled in the National School House on D'Auteuil street, but the situation had always proved inconvenient, moreover, a parish room, near to the Cathedral, wherein to hold meetings was found to be a necessity. The Cathedral Ladies' Guild was instituted at the instance of the Revd. C. W. Rawson, in 1881, and through its exertions the new Church Hall was erected with the Rector's permission, on the Rectory property on Garden street, having its main entrance on the Cathedral close.

The corner stone was laid on 4th June, 1890, by Mrs. Henry Russell, President of the Guild, to whose efforts were largely due the success of the movement for the erection of the new building. In the cavity under the stone, which forms the north east corner of the third course, were laid several newspapers of the day, including a copy of the *Chronicle*, a book of views of the city, several pieces of silver money and a parchment scroll with the following inscription :—" The corner stone of the Cathedral Church Hall " was duly laid on the 4th day of June, 1890, by Mrs. Henry " Russell, President of the Cathedral Ladies' Guild.

J. W., D.D., Bishop of the Diocese,
R. W. NORMAN, D.D., Dean of Quebec."

The solid silver trowel used on this occasion was presented to Mrs. Russell by the church wardens and Select Vestry, and the mallet by the contractors with this inscription on an inlaid silver plate :—" Made from a tree cut " down on the site of the Cathedral Hall, Quebec, 1890."

Besides the large hall the building contains committee and caretaker's rooms, and one set apart for the use of the Bishop.

The building was ready in the fall and the Sunday School was opened therein on the 9th November, 1890.

On the 28th June, 1793, was created the Diocese of Quebec, comprising the whole of Canada, with the exception of the Maritime Provinces. What changes have taken place during those hundred years? That same territory now contains the Dioceses of Quebec, Montreal, Ontario, Toronto, Niagara, Huron, Algoma and Ruperts Land. Bishop Mountain began his labors with nine clergymen to assist him, now that Ecclesiastical territory contains over 700 Ministers of the Church of England, and the cry is still for more.

Preparations have doubtless been already begun for celebrating in a suitable manner the Centennial of the Diocese of Quebec, and as a memorial thereof, if the history of the Diocese, as it now stands, as well as that of the dioceses combined in the original territory was written, an important link in the history of our Country would be thus placed on record.

APPENDIX A.

LETTERS PATENT ERECTING THE CATHEDRAL CHURCH
OF QUEBEC.

Signed,

ROBT. S. MILNES,

Lieut.-Governor.

George the Third, by the Grace of God, of the United
Kingdom of Great Britain and Ireland, King, Defender of
the Faith, &c.

To all to whom these presents shall come, Greeting :

WHEREAS, by Letters Patent under our great seal of
Great Britain, bearing date the twenty-eight day of June in
the thirty-third year of our reign, (1793). We did erect,
found, ordain, make and constitute our provinces of Lower
and Upper Canada and their dependencies to be a Bishop's
See, to be called from thenceforth the Bishoprick of Quebec.
—And whereas in Our pious regard for the Honor of
Almighty God and the good of souls, we have lately
caused to be built at Our expense in the city of Quebec in
Our said province of Lower Canada, in a certain square
there situated called the Parade or Place d'Armes, a
Church, of which said Church and of a certain Seite or lot
of land situate, lying and being contiguous to the said Church
in Our said City of Quebec, (on part whereof the said
Church is erected). We in right of our Crown are now,
seized in our Demesne as of Fee, the said seite or lot of land
being, fifty-five thousand and one hundred and fifty feet in
superficies. That is to say : Bounded on the north by St.
Anne's street, on the south by the vacant space between the
ground appropriated to the Court House and the said Church,
on the east by the Place d'Armes, and on the west by Garden
street. Beginning at twenty-five feet from the south-east
corner of Mr. Berthelot's house, which bears north ten
degrees, thirty minutes east from the corner of the wall or

place of departure. Running from thence magnetically south ten degrees thirty minutes east, one hundred and seventy-six feet, six inches along the division line or wall between the Place d'Armes and the Church premises, to the south-east corner of said lot, thence north seventy-seven degrees west along the south-west line of said premises, three hundred and nine feet, four inches, (which line is parallel to the Church wall at the distance of fifty-two feet six inches from it) including the breadth of the wall which divides Garden street, from the said premises, to the south-west corner of the same ; thence north seventeen degrees, thirty minutes west along the easterly side of Garden street, one hundred and eighty-six feet and a half, to the north-west corner of said lot or premises, and from thence south seventy three degrees, thirty minutes east, along the southerly side of St. Anne's street, two hundred and ninety-three feet and a half to the place of beginning.

Now wherefore know ye, that we have determined to erect the said Seite or lot of ground into an Episcopal Seat, and the said church into a Cathedral Church and by these presents we do create, erect, found, ordain make constitute and establish the said seite or lot of ground and Church aforesaid to be an Episcopal Seat and Cathedral church, for ever hereafter to be continue and remain the Episcopal Seat and Cathedral Church. And we do further by these presents create, erect, found, ordain, make, constitute and establish the said Cathedral Church to be the Cathedral Church of the said Bishoprick of Quebec, forever hereafter to be continue and remain the Cathedral Church of the said Bishoprick of Quebec, and forever hereafter to be called, known and distinguished by the name of the Cathedral Church of the Holy Trinity of the Bishoprick of Quebec.

And for us, our Heirs and Successors, we do hereby give, grant and confirm unto the Right Reverend father in God Jacob Mountain, now Bishop of the said Bishop's See of Quebec and to his successors Bishops of the said Bishop's

See of Quebec; the said Episcopal Seat and Cathedral Church
and their appurtenances respectively to have and to hold by
him the said Jacob Mountain, now Bishop of the said
Bishop's See of Quebec as aforesaid and his successors
Bishops of the said Bishop's See of Quebec from henceforth
forever.

And Our will and pleasure is and we do hereby ordain,
that the said Episcopal Seat and Cathedral Church shall
from henceforth forever be and remain the Episcopal Seat
and Cathedral Church of the said Jacob Mountain, Bishop
of the said Bishop's See of Quebec as aforesaid and his Successors Bishops of the said Bishop's See of Quebec and the
said Episcopal Seat and Cathedral Church, we do by these
presents invest with honors, dignities, preeminences and
distinctions of right belonging to an Episcopal Seat and
Cathedral Church.

Provided always and it is Our Royal intent and meaning,
that no house or other building or edifice whatsoever shall
at any time hereafter be erected on the said Scite or lot of
land or Episcopal Seat aforesaid, or on any part thereof, and
if any house or other building or edifice whatsoever shall
be at any time hereafter thereon or on any part thereof
erected by him the said Jacob Mountain, Bishop of the said
Bishop's See of Quebec, or by his successors Bishops of the
said Bishop's See of Quebec, or by any or either of them or
by his or their or either of their authority, sufferance or permission, then and in such case the said Scite and lot of land
or Episcopal Seat hereby granted and every part thereof
shall revert and escheat to us, our heirs and successors, and
shall thereupon become the absolute and entire property of
us and them in like manner as if the present grant had
never been made, anything herein contained to the contrary in anywise notwithstanding :

In testimony whereof, we have caused these our Letters
to be made Patent and the great seal of our said Province
of Lower Canada to be hereunto affixed.

Witness our trusty and beloved Sir Robert Shore Milnes, Baronet, Our Lieutenant-Governor of our said Province, at our Castle of Saint Lewis in our city of Quebec, in our said Province, the twenty-fifth day of August, in the year of Our Lord Christ, one thousand eight hundred and four, and in the forty-fourth year of our reign.

ROBT. S. MILNES,
Lieut.-Governor.

NATH. TAYLOR,
  Dept. Regr.

(L. S.)
  Fiat.

Recorded in the Register's office of the Records at Quebec, on Saturday the 15th day of September, 1804, in the second Register of Letters Patent of land Letter B, page 302.

NATH. TAYLOR,
Dept. Regr.

APPENDIX B.

SENTENCE OF CONSECRATION OF THE CATHE-DRAL AT QUEBEC, 28th AUGUST, 1804.

In the Name of God. Amen.

" Forasmuch as Our Sovereign Lord, George the Third,
" by the grace of God, of the United Kingdom of Great
" Britain and Ireland, King, defender of the faith, hath been
" piously disposed to erect and hath erected this the Cathe-
" dral Church of the Holy Trinity of the Bishoprick of
" Quebec to supply the spiritual wants of his people inha-
" bitants of the said Bishoprick. And the same hath pro-
" vided with a pulpit, reading desk, communion table, and
" all other things requisite for the decent performance of
" Divine Worship. And whereas our said Sovereign Lord
" the King, by Letters Patent under the great seal of Great
" Britain, bearing date the twenty-eight day of June, in the
" thirty-third year of his reign and by certain Letters
" Patent under the great seal of this province of Lower
" Canada bearing date the twenty-fifth day of August in-
" stant, the said Cathedral hath endowed. And whereas
" Sir George Pownall, Kt., the Hon. John Craigie, Esquire,
" Jonathan Sewell, Esquire, and Reverend Salter Jehosh-
" aphat Mountain, His Majesty's commissioners by him
" appointed for erecting the said Cathedral Church, have
" humbly notified unto us that the said Cathedral Church
" is completed and in a state fit in all things to be con-
" secrated, praying us to consecrate the same. Therefore,
" we Jacob by divine permission, Bishop of Quebec, do by
" our ordinary and episcopal authority set apart and forever
" separate this Cathedral Church so furnished, provided and
" endowed, from all common uses and do dedicate and con-
" secrate it forever to the service and worship of God,
" according to the rites of the Church of England, and

9

" we do hereby for ourselves and successors grant our
" consent and licence for the due celebration of Divine
" Worship in the said Cathedral Church, preaching the
" Word of God and the administration of the Holy Sacre-
" ments of the Lord's Supper and Baptism, and the ceremo-
" nies of marriage and burial of the dead. And we do hereby
" declare and decree this Cathedral Church to be appropriat-
" ed. dedicated and consecrated to God's worship, and that
" it shall so continue forever, reserving to ourselves and
" successors Bishops of Quebec (and to our Commissary and
" to all others acting under our authority,) full power to
" visit the said Cathedral Church as often as to us (or to
" them) shall seem proper and to enquire into, correct and
" punish according to the exigency of the Ecclesiastical laws
" of the realm all deviations from and offences against all
" other laws that now are or shall hereafter be made or
" enacted for the better security of the uniformity of public
" worship and finally to regulate all such matters as may
" appear to be amiss or to so want regulation in con-
" sequence of the neglect or misconduct of any minister
" officiating and of all other persons offending against the
" good order of Divine service within the said Cathedral
" Church. All which by this our definitive Sentence or
" final decree, we read and promulgate by these presents."

The above is the rough draft * of the sentence of consecration used by the Bishop. It seems that the original
document was lost, and on the 9th October, 1845, the Bishop
of Montreal caused the following certificate, signed by eye-
witness of the ceremony to be made and this rough draft,
which is extant, is the one mentioned in it :—

" Whereas it appears that the Cathedral Church of the
" city of Quebec was consecrated by the Right Reverend
" Jacob Mountain, D.D , Lord Bishop of Quebec, on the
" twenty-eighth day of August, in the year of our Lord, one

* In the Archives of the Cathedral.

" thousand eight hundred and four, (see the old *Quebec*
" *Gazette* of 6th September, 1804), by the name of the Cathe-
" dral Church of the Holy Trinity at Quebec, the petition in
" order to the performance of which ceremony is deposited
" of record in the said Cathedral Church, as also the original
" *rough* draft of the sentence of consecration read in the
" same ceremony. And whereas the sentence of consecra-
" tion duly executed under the Episcopal seal, as in such
" cases is wont to be done, cannot now, after diligent search,
" be found among the records and documents to the said
" Cathedral appertaining and belonging. And whereas it is
" expedient that sufficient evidence be recorded and pre-
" served of the fact of such ceremony having been duly and
" solemnly performed according to the manner received in
" the Church of England in that behalf: We therefore, the
" undersigned, do hereby, at the instance of the Right Rev-
" erend George Jehoshaphat Mountain, D.D., Lord Bishop of
" Montreal, administering the diocese of Quebec, certify and
" declare that we were present at the said ceremony per-
, " formed as aforesaid by the Right Reverend Jacob Moun-
" tain, D.D., Lord Bishop of Quebec, on the day and in the
" year above mentioned. Certain others of the clergy assist-
" ing therein, and a concourse of members of the Church
" being present. As witness our hands at Quebec, this
" ninth day of October, in the year of our Lord, one thou-
" sand eight hundred and forty-five."

Edward Bowen,	Mary Anne Mountain,
One of the Justices of	Eliza Scott,
the Queen's Bench	Sarah Montizambert,
for the district of Quebec.	Margaret Finlay,
	Jeremiah Wright,
	Retired Church clerk.
(L. S.)	Thomas Cary,
G. J. Montreal.	Church-warden
	of Quebec.

APPENDIX C.

BURIAL REGISTER OF THE DUKE OF RICHMOND.

" His grace Charles Duke of Richmond, Lenox and
" Aubigny, &c., &c., Knight of the most noble order of the
" Garter, Governor in Chief and Commander of the Forces in
" and over the British possessions in North America, aged
" fifty-five years, died at the new military settlement of
" Richmond, in Upper Canada, on the 29th August, and was
" buried in the Cathedral Church of Quebec, (this distinc-
" tion being by the Lord Bishop of the Diocese, specially
" and exclusively reserved for the representatives of His
" Majesty being Governors in Chief and dying in the execu-
" tion of their office,) on the 4th September, in the year of
" our Lord, 1819, by me,

J. QUEBEC,

Assisted by Geo. J. Mountain, officiating minister ;

Joseph Langley Mills,

Chaplain to the Forces.

Present :—W. MacLeod, Cousin, Major and Aide-de camp.
J. Ready, Lieut.-Col. and P. Secretary.
G. Bowles, Military Secretary and Major.
J. Harvey, Lieut.-Col., Dpy.-Adj.-Genl.
J. Sewell, Chief Justice of Lower Canada.
C. Marshall, Solicitor General, Lower Canada.
Ross Cuthbert, member Executive Council.
Wm Smith, member Executive Council.
John Caldwell, Receiver Genl. and member
Legislature of Canada.

www.ingramcontent.com/pod-product-compliance
Lightning Source LLC
Chambersburg PA
CBHW021529270326
41930CB00008B/1155